Martyrs and Chickens

The DreamSeeker Memoir Series

On an occasional and highly selective basis, books in the DreamSeeker Memoir Series, intended to make available fine memoirs by writers whose works at least implicitly arise from or engage Anabaptist-related contexts, themes, or interests, are published by Cascadia Publishing House LLC under the DreamSeeker Books imprint. Cascadia oversees content of these novels or story collections in collaboration with DreamSeeker Memoir Series Editor Jeff Gundy.

1. Yoder School
   By Phyllis Miller Swartz, 2019
2. East of Liberal: Notes on the Land
   By Raylene Hinz-Penner, 2022
3. New Moves: A Theological Odyssey
   By J. Denny Weaver, 2023
4. Martyrs and Chickens:
   Confessions of a Granola Mennonite
   By Kirsten Eve Beachy, 2025

Martyrs and Chickens

Confessions of a Granola Mennonite

a memoir by

Kirsten Eve Beachy

DreamSeeker Memoir Series, Volume 4

DreamSeeker Books
TELFORD, PENNSYLVANIA

an imprint of
Cascadia Publishing House LLC

Cascadia Publishing House orders, information, reprint permissions:
contact@CascadiaPublishingHouse.com
1-215-723-9125
126 Klingerman Road, Telford PA 18969
www.CascadiaPublishingHouse.com

Martyrs and Chickens
Copyright © 2025 by Cascadia Publishing House LLC
Telford, PA 18969
All rights reserved
DreamSeeker Books is an imprint of Cascadia Publishing House LLC
ISBN 13: 978-1-68027-025-9

Book design by Cascadia Publishing House
Cover design by Gwen M. Stamm
Photos of Kirsten Eve Beachy and chickens by Tiffany Showalter

Library of Congress Cataloging-in-Publication Data

Names: Beachy, Kirsten, 1979- author.
Title: Martyrs and chickens : confessions of a granola Mennonite / a memoir by Kirsten Eve Beachy.
Description: Telford, Pennsylvania : DreamSeeker Books, an imprint of Cascadia Publishing House LLC, 2025. | Series: DreamSeeker memoir series ; volume 4 | Includes bibliographical references. | Summary: "In the essays comprising this memoir, Beachy wonders what a martyr heritage means for herself and her children, celebrates the complexities of simple living, philosophizes on chickens and more, and seeks balance as artist and caregiver"-- Provided by publisher.
Identifiers: LCCN 2024056307 | ISBN 9781680270259 (trade paperback)
Subjects: LCSH: Beachy, Kirsten, 1979- | Mennonite women authors--United States--Biography. | Women college teachers--United States--Biography.
Classification: LCC BX8143.B375 A3 2025 | DDC 289.7092 [B]--dc23/eng/20250110
LC record available at https://lccn.loc.gov/2024056307

*To
Mom and Dad
and to
Jason,
of course*

Contents

1 Invocation to the Martyrs and Chickens   13
2 Notes to Myself   17
3 Corn Day   21
4 Me and the Martyrs   29
5 Milk   41
6 Amish Country   48
7 Selling the Farm   56
8 House   74
9 A Butcher of Conscience   89
10 The Last Worker   95
11 Field Notes Towards a Doctrine of Chicken   99
12 Eggs: A Short History of Infertility and Ducks   108
13 The Fathers   117
14 The Voice   122
15 Mennonite Girls Can Read (With Recipes!)   125
16 Walking   131
17 C is for Clomid   136
18 Lavish Banquets   144
19 Honey   147

20 Written On I   150
21 Notes from the Night Owl Feed   156
22 To the (Unattributed) Mennonite Pastor Who Said that Children Are for Martyrdom   165
23 Written On II   178
24 Woman Built of Stones:
    A Mother Tries to Write   181
25 Salt   189
26 Simple   198

Gratitudes   219
Credits   223
Notes   225
The Author   227

You can be a mother and a poet. A wife and a lover. You can dance on the graves you dug on Tuesday, pulling out the bones of yourself you began to miss.

—Kate Baer

1

Invocation to the Martyrs and the Chickens

The sun creeps down my office wall this morning, and when the 8:30 alarm sounds on my phone, I'll take a yellow dot sticker and pin it to the corner of the rectangle of sun _____ against the wall. What's the word I want? I think of typing "splashed against the wall" as a placeholder, but that's not the right verb at all. I'm rusty. The sun through the window is falling on, or maybe leaning against, the wall, but not even that—it's shivering and dappled with leaf shadows, and slipping swiftly down, even as I press my thumb to the sticker. I have to be prompt to catch the corner at this moment. In September, the morning sun shifts so fast, and every day it lands in a new spot at the appointed time. A ragged line of dots on my desk marks its August path. It's a good use of office supplies, I think, tracking the earth and the sun in their reliable dance; they persist no matter what's on my to-do list, how well I'm sleeping, which forests are burning, or who is running the local school board.

At the window sill, a post-it note records my daily count of magnolia blossoms on the trees outside. It's been so dry, they've stopped unfolding their silk white blooms—or maybe magnolias don't bloom in Harrisonburg in September. On the most extravagant day in August, I counted nine of them opening, but this week the count holds steady at zero.

I try to read a poem each day when I come into the office, unless there's somewhere I have to be immediately. I take it like a dose of medicine, like the preventive shot of elderberry I give my daughter Sallie every morning to boost her slow immune system. Today's poem comes from Luisa Igloria's collection *The Buddha Wonders if She is Having a Mid-Life Crisis*. It is an apt title. I did not expect that I would need to be so systematic in fighting despair (which I know is a luxury) in this season of life. I have many care-giving duties but plenty of resources; I have been working too hard through the pandemic years but have carved out a space in this season with fewer duties and release time for writing at my academic job.

Before the children were born, words were my work and my joy. As I read back through the stories I told at that time, I am not even sure I recognize my voice. I'm not so clever any more; I have more doubts, more understanding of my power and my responsibility and my ignorance, too. It's been so long since I've shared myself in writing that I hesitate to get started with the project of linking together memories from across more than twenty years, and across long gaps in time.

Will the magic still be there?

I made a commitment to pick up my work this fall. All through my summer break, perhaps in preparation, I lost myself in wonderful stories, women's stories, speculative fiction about dragons and space, time travel and transformation. I tried to, but couldn't, pay attention to the craft of their writing. Instead, I sank myself deep into other people's imagined lives, other people's histories.

I am privileged to be able to trace my family history for generations, to know I'm descended from a martyr people. Martyrs speak across the ages—they testify, they write with their lives. I, too, have the impulse to testify, but at my core I'm more backyard hen than principled resister. Chickens dust bathe in sunny corners, scratch for beetles, stay close to the roost. I used to keep chickens, before I kept children. My parents, Mennonites who came of age in the late sixties, that first generation of Granola

15 Martyrs and Chickens

Mennonites who went from head coverings to bell bottoms, taught me our history and gave me my first little chicken.

I like to stay where it's warm, comfortable. I like to hide inside other people's writing. I'm usually quiet until I say too much, all in a rush, probably on top of someone else's story. Nevertheless, I'll try to tell the truth in this book, however it meets me as I spiral around each memory in each revision, wondering how best to preserve them—pin them like specimens? Etch them like engravings? Boil them with sugar until they gel? Blanch them, scrape off the kernels, and drop them in the deep freeze? Pluck, gut, and roast them? And now I'm too far adrift in metaphor, which is not a bad place to find yourself, any morning.

The sun has fallen off the wall and slips silently across the floor.

*

Dear martyrs, dearest chickens,
as I visit each earlier version of my self,
let me honor her language and thoughts.
Keep me open to my fluid and doubtful sense of self,
my roadrunner heart
the wrong turns that turned out right
or wrong anyway.

Let my touch be light
as I bring these old works together into one story.
When I come to the gaps in chronology,
the spaces where I could not write,
let me document the images and memories that linger
with compassion.

Help me remember how to be clever and bold and wise
*   and authentic,*
to tell the truth, the whole truth, and make it interesting

—at least the parts that are mine to tell.

Please, please, please
let something happen when I open an empty page and
offer it my time.

2

Notes to Myself

Morgantown, West Virginia

Someday it will happen: one of your colleagues—say, the woman who teaches First-Year Composition in the classroom down the hall from you—will ask the question. It's best to answer without pausing. Tell her you're Mennonite. As she squints over your shoulder, looking for the horse and buggy, clarify. Say there are all sorts of Mennonites, but you're a modern Mennonite. Better yet, postmodern. After all, you've got a liberal arts education, cable Internet, and subscriptions to *The New Yorker* and *Scientific American*.

Resist the urge to blab cultural details. Do not mention the kitchen drawer full of recycled twist-ties, the compulsion to turn off all unused lights and appliances, the guilt you feel at throwing away used egg cartons because there just isn't enough cabinet space in your grad-student rental. Make no allusion to the bacon-craving peasant at war with the granola-making vegetarian in your soul. Say: "It's not so different from any modern religious group."

If she presses for more, go with doctrine. Pick two unique features that appeal to you: Peace. Service. Use peripheral vision to gauge her comfort at speaking with a dutiful idealist. Do not pursue the subject unless she prompts you. Remember: You don't like to talk about yourself.

If she toured Amish country last July and sees you as a link to a world of charm and simplicity, she might want to go out for a drink and discuss it more. Wait until you get to the bar to tell her that despite all your German DNA, you don't know how to drink. Order cranberry juice.

Start with some history. Tell her that Mennonites and Amish are so interwoven it doesn't much matter which group split off from the other. They decided the Reformation needed reforming, that "love your neighbor" meant renouncing violence. They rebaptized their members, who were subsequently martyred in gruesome ways.

Buy your companion another beer before you continue. Share the stories that raised goosebumps on your childhood vertebrae. Tell about your predecessors burnt, drowned, and hung in cages for the birds and the spectacle. Don't forget: Dirk Willems, who escaped from prison across the thin ice of a pond, but turned back to rescue the pursuer who broke through. Burnt. Maeyken Wens, who was so persuasive the authorities clamped her tongue with a tongue screw so she couldn't evangelize on her way to her death. Also burnt. Admire, but do not mention, your companion's tongue piercing.

Change the subject to something else you like: hymns. You grew up singing four-part harmony, usually a cappella. Even now that you think you know better, you love to belt out the hymns, especially the ones with blood in them, full of male pronouns for God. There's music in your blood. Great-Grandpa composed hymns on his organ until the elders decreed that musical instruments were too worldly. After the organ was sent away, he lined up his five children and made them sing the notes in his head. But the children were rarely available—the family stories have them busy stringing secret radio antennae under the kitchen table and flinging tomatoes at the neighbor's chickens. Great-Grandpa stopped writing music. The elders were concerned. Why had he stopped composing? With their permission but under cover of darkness, Great-Grandpa hitched up the wagon and brought home his organ.

In the next generation, one set of grandparents left their childhood farms to do missionary radio overseas, the other grandparents watched their dairy farm disappear beneath housing developments. Your own parents: a chimney sweep-turned-computer analyst and a stay-at-home mom with secret writing aspirations. All of them Mennonite.

If you feel reckless, let your interrogator get you a drink with actual alcohol in it. Go for something sweet and fruity. Make a joke about girly drinks. Don't close your eyes when you sip. After your stomach is warm, decide. Will you talk about yourself? If she's not fiddling with her watch, plunge in. Tell about growing up without television and scared of movies, even Bambi. Encountering an unknown character you called Dark Vader in the school yard. Sitting under the quilt at Homemaker's Fellowship while old women stitched impossible stitches, wearing thimbles to protect their fingers from the tiny needles and coverings to protect their heads from sin. The hymn sings you'd have some Sunday evenings when the Black church joined you and the singing got so fast and loud that some of those old women forgot themselves and swayed.

Don't tell your companion how many different ways you and your husband are sixth cousins. Don't tell about your aunt's twelve toes. Don't try to explain your attraction to fresh turnips, your secret longings for chickens that lay green eggs. Don't describe your own baptism, twelve years old, in a mix of glory and shyness and confusion. Instead, drain your glass. Tell your friend that you went to a family reunion this summer. Tell her there's this song you sang. Everywhere your kind of Mennonites gather, this song is sung. You've heard it at Seaworld. In the Metro. They sang it at your parents' wedding. Your own. 606 in the old red hymnal. 118 in the new blue one.[1] Grab her sleeve. Lean in. Say, "I'm going to sing it to you."

Glance around, then start in a whisper.
Praise God from whom all blessings flow
Praise him all creatures here below,
Praise him above, ye heavenly host.

Overturn your glass. Shout, "the heck with it!" No. Shout, "the *hell* with it!"

Stand on your stool. Belt it out.
Praise Father, Son, and Holy Ghost,

Try to sing all the parts, breathlessly leaping between the bass rumbling up, altos blending, sopranos going it alone on top, tenors taking their time, *hallelujahs* intertwining, *amens* in punctuation.

Hallelujah Amen, Hallelujah, Amen.

3

Corn Day

Brunswick County, Virginia

On the dark back roads of central Virginia, I'm driving south to corn day at my in-laws' farm with Jason, my husband of six months. His father Harold was born on the Warwick River in a Mennonite farming colony called Denbigh, now part of the spreading city of Newport News. By the time Harold was old enough to work on a farm—all he wanted in life—he had to move inland to Powhatan County; when he was ready to start his own dairy farm, he had to migrate down to the North Carolina border to find land that still sold for farms and not subdivisions.

It's eight hours to the Alderfer farm from our apartment in Morgantown, West Virginia. The roads through the mountains run southwest along the valleys, so we have to drive against our goal until we find gaps that allow eastern passage. If a crow could fly to Harold and Elaine's without perishing in the Alleghenies, it would reach the farm in half the miles we must drive.

I drive while Jason stares out glassy-eyed. For two years, he has enthused about Corn Day: the rows of sweet corn planted along the edge of the field corn, the fat ears, the huge outdoor cooker, the vats of ice-water in the milkroom for cooling corn, the slicer-creamer that strips a corn cob bare in a few strokes. But tonight he's less animated than your average zombie. Perhaps because he spent the morning rushing to finish his telecommuting projects, perhaps because of our fast-food supper. It wasn't real food.

Around midnight, we pull off Dry Bread Road and into the farm lane. From the front, the old farmhouse is dark save one light at the top of the stairs, but around back, the kitchen blazes with light. As I climb from the car, damp heat beads under my arms, and the air is too heavy to breathe. Suddenly I recall the hot summers when I was a child growing up in those suburbs that once were Denbigh, Virginia, years after Jason's father began his farming migration. We moved north before I turned ten, so I always believed the Virginia summer heat had been exaggerated by childishness and that I had grown out of minding high temperatures. Yet here it is, even in the middle of the night, waiting for me: those days when we were dragged from the cool spaces in front of the box fan, or from under the shade of trees, out to weed the garden where sun baked the sandy soil. How I hated the forced labor of the garden, how I looked forward to the day when I would leave it behind. Now, with only a lawnmower-width strip of grass on each side of our rental place, I long for garden-growing space.

We escape the heat and go into the kitchen, where the house is silent except for the constant chug of the window air conditioner. Sometimes when we arrive late, Harold lies in the den recliner, snoring to shake the house, napping before his final inspection of the cow-lot. But tonight all is still.

It's hard to believe that only a few months ago this house was the cacophonous scene of an Easter Saturday gathering of the Alderfers—Jason's aunts and uncles and their children and grandchildren—the get-together fortified by his mother Elaine's baked ham and hot pans of creamed sweet corn; people who knew nothing better than talking, clogging the halls and the den and the stairwells with their conversation. It was impossible to walk from the living room to the dining room, from the library through the office to the kitchen without pulling in and out of five different discussions. The house seems smaller tonight without the belated unwrapping of wedding presents in odd corners, the surprise cake for Aunt Sarah's birthday, the impromptu concert from the musical cousins (the girls in conservative long hair and dresses, the oldest with her head covered in a modest kerchief), the picture-taking that was never complete because someone was going for a walk or putting the baby to sleep or looking for cousin Raymond who was looking for them or climbing the silo or waking the baby up for the picture or looking for the good camera.

We seal the air-conditioned part of the house behind us and tiptoe upstairs to Jason's old room. Elaine left a fan blowing the night air through the window, but even on the highest setting it can't compensate for the torrid state of the air. Jason, hot-blooded, has to stand in front of the fan for a long time before he is cool enough to crawl under the sheet in the four-poster bed.

On another visit, almost this late at night, Harold came in from checking the cows and told Jason he had one down with milk fever, a calcium deficiency that can kill cows that have just calved. I donned rubber boots and held the light while the men injected calcium into the fallen cow's neck. In moments, the dull skin of despair evaporated from her eyes and soon we coaxed her to her feet. Tonight, though, no one interrupts our sleep.

I hurry down the stairs a little before eight the next morning, early for me but late for Elaine, who got up at 3:30 to milk a hundred cows. She heads out the door in a bright pink sun hat as I sit down to a bowl of homemade granola and fresh milk. She disappears down the lane in the pick-up truck to pick corn. The sun is already merciless. I find an old shirt to protect my arms from the itchy cornfield and set out on foot toward Brown's Creek Road, where Jason said that Harold usually plants the sweet corn.

Down the dusty, rutted lane the crepe myrtles lift purple blooms on branches sleek and sinewy, like yoga masters. I don't stop to admire them today, but swerve off into the field. The corn grows high, but it all looks the same; it must be field corn. There's no white truck and no answer to my shouts, so I try the next field, hunting the sweet corn. In the shade of the tree border, some of the puddles in the deepest tractor ruts haven't yet dried up, and frogs splash across them, croaking alarms as I pass. At the end of the next wide field, I holler again, then give up. Somewhere, Elaine is slaving alone in the corn.

I start back up the lane to the house, this same lane that Cowboy fish-tailed his pickup into, driving one-handed the day he cut off his thumb. Cowboy raised horses, wore a western-style hat and boots, and insisted on being called Cowboy. As Harold tells it, he laid on the horn until Harold came running.

Harold took one look at the thumb sawed clean through the bone and jumped into the truck. "Get over!" he said. He wanted to drive Cowboy to the emergency room.

But Cowboy refused. "Get Elaine out here to fix it up."

Plead as they might, the Alderfers couldn't get him to see a doctor. Elaine poured peroxide over the wound and splinted it up with adhesive, possibly duct tape, and Cowboy went on his way. The thumb healed up—and worked. They say he dosed himself with horse medicine.

I remind myself I am searching for sweet corn, not stories, today.

Back at the machine shed, Jason digs up a board for our worktable. When I tell him I can't find the sweet corn patch, he scans the fields like a farmer, squinting his eyes against the sun, and I see where his crow's-feet came from. He walks me out to the proper field with the pink-tasseled sweet corn. The pickup is in a clear corridor between a wall of still-ripening field corn and the stand of heavy-eared sweet corn. As I reach it, the pink hat emerges with Elaine under it, her five gallon bucket stuffed with ears wrapped tight in their husks. "I didn't know you were coming to help," she says. That's the delightful thing about Elaine. She works hard but doesn't think less of you if you don't.

Heavy rains made this corn shoot up before Harold could cultivate the weeds between the rows. As I plunge in with my bucket, weeds that I'd met in inch-sized versions as a child in Mom's garden burgeon higher than my head. I trample some and dodge between the others. Orgies of Japanese beetles gather on isolated ears, chewing straight down to the cob. I meet Elaine pouring corn into the truck bed when I emerge from the jungle and ask how many ears we need. She isn't sure, but she's aiming for a hundred pints of creamed corn this year. We stop picking when the heat becomes unbearable and drive back to the house.

The blue Harvestor silos reflect the morning sun. We've climbed the highest one several times—ninety feet into the sky. Jason climbs it to replace the bulbs in the Christmas star and once to fly our kite when there was no wind at ground level. Another time, we scaled it together at the start of evening to watch the sun slip away from the fields spread below, the cattle coming up the lane to the barn, the corrugated roofs of the machine sheds and dairy, the farmhouse and rose garden, Aunt Lorraine's trailer, the vegetable garden, the cats waking, the guinea hens going to roost in the magnolia tree, and right beneath us, a flock of geese flying past on their way to the far farm pond.

We back the truck under the pecan tree, where a breeze and the mysterious out-breathings of the tree cool the air. Jason, Harold, and I perch on the back of the pick-up to husk corn. Aunt Lorraine, who lives by the pond and does the afternoon milking, unpacks her chair, knife, and vegetable brush beside us and says, "I don't know how long I can help out without a system." She doesn't expect we'll hold out long sitting on the tailgate, and I'm blocking the corn in the truck. But soon we've configured the chairs and baskets and she settles into an efficient husking routine.

Inside the tip of each husk is a green worm gnawing away. My goal, I announce, is to get through the day without dropping a worm on my leg. Immediately, one falls out of the ear I'm husking and bites my thigh. The only thing more horrifying than a corn worm is a squished corn worm, or one that's broken in half. I grow careful. What is it about love that later makes me dangle a worm over Jason?

Harold called various neighbors looking for a kitchen timer we could use to clock the blanching, so folks keep stopping by to bring us timers and stay to tell us who's sick or dying or dead or just born. Harold and Elaine send them away with arm-loads of corn or direct them out to the field where they can pick all they want. We taste our first ears at lunch, but before we go inside we cover the stainless steel bowls of husked ears with cloths—already the flies are thick. It's the sweetness of the corn that attracts them. They settle in clouds on the discarded husks. Often when I was a child, at the end of a day picking blueberries or processing peaches, I would see the fruit again on the backs of my eyelids. Tonight instead of corn I will see black fly spots buzzing and milling across my vision until I fall asleep.

After lunch, I husk with Harold. A full stomach, the intensified afternoon heat, and the relentless schedule of a farmer are taking their toll. I can tell he's almost gone when he drops ears hairy with silk into the bowl. I try to keep him talking, but the ear in his hand soon dips. He tries valiantly to lift it and pick off the silk, but it dips again. After about four repetitions, he drops it. This wakes him up, and he resumes husking. When Harold is not working or eating or telling stories, he is sleeping. Once the urge to sleep overcame him while he was in the field, and he shut down the tractor and took a nap on the wheel, to the dismay of a neighbor, who ran out hollering, "Mr. Aldafuh? Is you all right?"

Elaine strides past on her way to the house with the first ten pints of corn sealed in freezer bags. When the last ear is husked, I join her in the milk room. There, we receive the steaming ears that Jason boils in the cooker outside, twenty-five at a time. We plunge them in a succession of waters from cool to icy. When they have cooled, we scrape the corn on the toothed creamer. Elaine has scraped thirty pints with a pain in her back, so I take charge of the creamer and tell her to go in and rest. "But it's corn day!" she protests, and starts filling bags. The first few strokes on the creamer are awkward, but soon I develop a rhythm: *turn, scrape, scrape; turn, scrape scrape*—in my mind, I waltz "The Blue Danube."

Harold once had a pain in his side bad enough to send him to the doctor, who said he'd strained a muscle and should rest. There is no time to rest on a dairy, but after a week Harold felt so poorly he laid out on lounge chair in the yard while he waited for the vet to come see some cows. He thought he'd make a joke of it and tried to look like he was dying when the vet came. Beecher Junior had barely shut the car door before he said, "You look awful. What's wrong with you?"

Harold told him it was a bad muscle.

"Where does it hurt?"

Harold showed him.

"That's no pulled muscle. It's either appendicitis or gall bladder."

Harold said he was fine, actually, but the vet told him, "You get to the emergency room or it'll be your funeral."

The part about the funeral got Harold's attention, and that evening after work he checked into the hospital. He stayed for a week. His appendix had ruptured, but he didn't die because he's made of leather and steel and full of Elaine's healthy meals, and the vet caught it just in time. The doctor who told him it was a pulled muscle lost his license to practice.

The vet was modest about his life-saving diagnosis: "It was easy enough. Most of my patients can't even talk."

By five o'clock we have processed a scant forty pints and the pile of ears seems as high as ever. A dozen flies slip through the milk room door and make a playground of our work table. One sneaks into an open freezer bag and Elaine scolds, but can't catch it. Back pain notwithstanding, Elaine decides that she will blanch corn on the porch stove to speed up the process. Jason thinks we can get the cooker hotter if he can fix a broken regulator on the propane tank. He goes off to tinker, leaving the corn unattended. Of course it begins to boil, and alone in the milk room, peering through the screen door at the steaming pot, I scrape cobs like a madwoman, trying to keep up with the corn Elaine brings from the porch. Fifty pints. Sixty. *Turn, scrape, scrape; turn, scrape, scrape.* Jason wizards a gasket and the cooker heats twice as fast. It's past seven, but we're going flat out and can't stop now. Seventy pints. Eighty. Elaine takes over for a minute while I step outside with Jason and do stretches to relax my corn-scraping arm.

Our evening walks often end here at the milk room so we can hose off our boots and wash our hands by the giant stainless steel holding tank, the vats of cleaning acid strong enough to burn your flesh off your bones, the liquid nitrogen tank chilling pipettes of semen for artificial insemination. The little room is bright against the evening dusk. Once I walked all evening around the flower beds with Jason as he talked about his love for the land, the hard work his parents endure, the easy life he leads with his computer work, forty-hour work week, and suburban apartment. Missing the farm and wondering what will become of it, wishing he could be here to help bring in the crops, to bear the weight of drought years, to use his expertise to fix the machines and keep up the buildings—the work one man can't do alone. Jason is the only child, the heir apparent, but he will not be a dairy man.

It was in this milk room that I whispered into his shirt words that I wouldn't say aloud for months—that I wanted to carry this past with him. My mother grew up on a dairy farm on the Warwick River, in that same green colony of Mennonites where Harold was born, before it became city. This is my chance to come to an old home and lose it again, to stop and listen to the pulse of the land in my blood, at least a moment, and decide with Jason how to build life in relation to it.

Inside, Elaine worries about the gathering clouds. We hear the thunder rumbling in the distance. No. It's Jason outside the window, shaking a piece of aluminum sheeting. When his theatrics are finished, he rigs a roof for his work, protecting it from the shower that stays for a few dust-dampening moments. We pass one hundred pints and Elaine's bedtime, but the corn keeps coming. It's 8:30 before we scrape the last ear—one hundred and twenty pints, exactly. The rest of us clean the milk room as Elaine makes supper. The mountain of husks under the pecan tree is gone: Aunt Lorraine took them to the heifers as a treat.

Elaine cooks eight ears of corn to go with the chicken, but no one can manage more than one. "Just throw those others away," she says, and finally agrees to go to bed after we promise we can clean up the kitchen without her. "I love you *all*," she sighs on her way to the stairs.

The next morning, she congratulates Jason for finding a wife who can survive corn day, and I feel that I've passed an important test. Off we go, leaving the freezer sweating as it cools the corn. Next visit, the corn will be thoroughly frozen, and we'll fill an ice chest to take back to Morgantown with us. Even amid suburban apartments and one-way streets, with sirens wailing under our living room window, we'll taste hot, sweet summer on our tongues.

4

Me and the Martyrs

Morgantown, West Virginia

In our first year of marriage, the *Martyrs Mirror* crowned the pile of genealogical charts, family histories, and half-written manuscripts in the tiny office in our apartment in Morgantown. The book details torments endured by Anabaptists and their predecessors all the way back to Christ—burnings, drownings, and more creative torture. Which surprises you more: that the *Martyrs Mirror* came to me and Jason as a wedding present or that we put it on our gift registry along with the *Moosewood Cookbook*?

Jason's aunt bought it for us. Maybe she got it at a discount through her library connections; if so, we're proud of her. That thrift proves we're Mennonite: When a Mennonite dies, someone else has to find a use for the empty yogurt containers, the drawers full of salvaged ziploc bags. I can't throw out food; sour milk waits at the back of my fridge because I hope to bake it into something, sometime. Our people saw long years of suffering. Generations later, we're still stocking up, just in case there's another round of persecution, another bloody theater.

That's the full name of the book by Thieleman J. van Braght: *The Bloody Theater or Martyrs Mirror of the Defenseless Christians: Who Baptized Only Upon Confession of Faith, and Who Suffered and Died for the Testimony of Jesus, Their Savior, From the Time of Christ to the Year A.D. 1660*. First published in Dutch, it is as heavy as a library dictionary. If I needed a break or Jason's head hurt from telecommuting, we could brew some tea and read the letters and court records, pore over the pictures. We might open the book to a vivid engraving by Jan Luyken, like the print of Ursel van Essen. She hangs by her bound wrists from a post, naked toes dangling a foot above the ground, back bared, while a man flails her with bundles of branches, one in each hand. In the background, a dozen men in fine hats watch.

Van Braght, with painstaking attention to detail, explains that before Ursel's 1570 imprisonment, she was so "tender of body" that "she had to turn her stockings inside out, and put them on and wear them thus, because she could not bear the seams of the stockings inside on her limbs." Tender-bodied Ursel endured the scourging twice and the rack repeatedly, refusing to renounce her faith. Reading, we were careful not to spill our tea on the pages.

Who were these Anabaptists? Who am I? It's taken me years to straighten out the story of these radicals who tried to reform the Reformation and as a result were despised by both Catholics and Protestants: When Martin Luther nailed his ninety-five theses to the door of Wittenberg church in 1517, priests and laity across Europe joined him in questioning the Roman Catholic church. While Luther was content to reform the state church, some radicals wanted to depart entirely from state-sponsored religion and return to what they believed were the practices of the original church.

Anabaptism began, some say, in Zurich in 1525 when Conrad Grebel baptized George Blaurock. Others place the beginning two years later, with Michael Sattler's Schleitheim confession, which delineated key beliefs: baptism of repentant adults, renunciation of the sword, and separation from the world. Thieleman J. van Braght of the *Martyrs Mirror* traces Anabaptism directly to Christ through various incarnations of the "true" church, whose members were often vigorously persecuted.

The authorities imprisoned Grebel for life; he managed to escape. He soon died of the plague and so is not listed with van Braght's martyrs. Sattler's trial and letters, however, hold a prominent place in the *Martyrs Mirror,* for his persecutors cut out his tongue, tore him repeatedly with red hot tongs, and then burned him to ashes. A few days afterward, they burned his wife because she, too, refused to recant. Blaurock also ended in flames.

Persecution only encouraged the spread of Anabaptism. The Anabaptists who survived the ideological purges fled to Alsace, the Netherlands, Moravia, and the Palatinate. In the Netherlands and northern Germany, Menno Simons, an ex-Catholic priest, emerged as a leader and became well known for teachings like this:

> For true evangelical faith is of such a nature that it cannot lay dormant; but manifests itself in all righteousness and works of love; it dies unto flesh and blood; destroys all forbidden lusts and desires; cordially seeks, serves and fears God; clothes the naked; feeds the hungry; consoles the afflicted; shelters the miserable; aids and consoles all the oppressed; returns good for evil; serves those that injure it; prays for those that persecute it; teaches, admonishes and reproves with the Word of the Lord; seeks that which is lost; binds up that which is wounded; heals that which is diseased and saves that which is sound.[2]

Despite a bounty on his head (which included full pardon for murderers), Menno lived to die of old age. His followers took, or were given, his name. The Amish developed from the Swiss Mennonite tradition; the groups that fled to Moravia became Hutterites. Other denominations have been called Anabaptist for their approaches to baptism but are not historically descended from the martyrs of the *Mirror*.

Today the North American descendants of the Anabaptists range from Amish groups who farm with draft horses and pray in German dialects, to members of Hutterite communities who keep their possessions in common, to modern Mennonite congregations who sing choruses glowing on the wall in Powerpoint projections. More Mennonites have churches in the global south than in the northern hemisphere, so global expressions of the faith extend even further.

In Morgantown, Jason and I drove an hour each week to attend a house church where communion was a potluck, volunteers signed up on a clipboard to give sermons, activism and wisdom were primary concerns, and John Denver songs mingled with four-part hymns. I wear blue jeans but feel kinship when I pass an Amish buggy on the road. There is a deep though tenuous connection between us, in our blood, in our combined relatedness to the martyrs.

Modern Mennonites avoid war but like to send food and blankets to war-torn countries. When gruesome battle images appear on our televisions, we turn them off. My fascination with the bloody martyrs is out of vogue. The *Martyrs Mirror* was once considered the perfect wedding gift, but I got odd looks from folks when I asked for one. It's okay to use small excerpts in Sunday school materials, or to study the book if you're a scholar, but it's rather suspect to read it at leisure.

It's fine, however, to want to know your origins, so I could write it off as interest in my heritage. Jason has a keen taste for genealogy. Sometimes I would turn from my desk to catch him surfing Amish genealogical databases instead of grooming email servers and firewalls. His exploration started during our engagement, as a search to see whether we were related. It turns out we're sixth cousins and share many forebears. We collect their stories.

The best-known story of an ancestor we share—a story I shall return to—is the tale of Jacob Hostetler and the Indian raid. In the classic version of this story by William F. Hochstetler,[3] Jacob and his wife arrived in Philadelphia on the ship *Harle* in 1736, made their way to what is now Berks County, Pennsylvania, and carved a farm out of the forest. The raid occurred twenty years later, during the French and Indian War. The family refused to defend themselves. The attackers captured Jacob and two of his sons but murdered the mother and two other children. Multiple accounts of the raid exist: blood ensures a history will be handed down.

I recognized the Hostetler story as one my father had told me and my sister when we were little girls. Mom read us fairy tales and the Bible and *Heidi*, but Dad told us our history. We didn't have the *Martyrs Mirror*, but he made sure we knew about Maeyken Wens of Antwerp, who refused to renounce her beliefs and was burnt in 1573. They clamped her tongue with a specially fitted screw to prevent her singing hymns or preaching heresies. Her son stood on a bench at the back of the crowd, but the sight overcame him and he fainted. Afterwards, he sifted the ashes and, finding no trace of her body, kept the screw. A century later, as van Braght compiled the stories, he knew of this souvenir. Perhaps he even saw it; perhaps he held it in his hand. I thought my father had seen it, too. He held out his hand, empty, and we imagined the cruel screw nesting inside.

I was a child among Virginia Mennonites whose old women covered their heads in church and let me sit under their quilts at Homemaker's Fellowship. When I was ten, we moved to small-town southern Indiana. Some of my Amish fifth cousins farmed surrounding hills but we didn't visit them. The local Mennonites wore blue jeans and Indian prints; they were granola-making, talkative coffee addicts. They baptized me amid my awkward adolescence. I burned with embarrassment as the water dripped from my head onto my green suede skirt, as everyone who could reach into the circle laid their hands upon my shoulders, my back, my arms, even my feet. Shy, I wanted to be done with it quickly. The ritual of baptism was necessary to be baptized, to be a permanent member of the community. I was old enough to know what I believed and where I belonged, but too young to be proud of it, to do more than stammer the necessary words.

Over the years, our Sunday school materials and church bulletins featured one engraving from the *Martyrs Mirror* that didn't portray immediate gore. In the foreground, Dirk Willems, in broad-brimmed hat and billowing frock coat, kneels on the ice of a frozen river, his hands outstretched to a man struggling in open water. There's urgency in Willems' stance: he has been running, but this final reach must be careful. The arms of the drowning man stretch toward his arms; the white space where they almost meet is full of tension.

We learned that Dirk Willems, condemned for his beliefs, escaping across a frozen river, turned back to rescue his pursuer. Afterwards, he was taken into custody, tried, and burned on another blustery day, a day too windy for the fire to burn properly; he died a lingering death, calling out to God again and again. These horrors did not distress me. They seemed necessary, inevitable as the closing of white space between the arms of rescuer and supplicant. My ancestors could not cast off their beliefs.

Perhaps because of this steadfastness, schisms are not uncommon among Anabaptists. It is so important to be right, to be the true church, that our communities splinter to protect the pure from contamination. It's surprising I haven't split off from the church myself. Instead, I've embedded myself in a small church, a sprout from the tree of the Mennonites that accepts doctrine-wary dreamers. If someone tried to shun me, I wouldn't go.

The distance between me and the martyrs is a comfortable one. I can imagine them from afar like classical heroes. I don't know whether any of the martyrs in the book are my ancestors—we moved and lost so much, left generations behind on the journey across the Atlantic, lost too many stories in the translation from German to English. We have no souvenirs to hold. There is a wide, white space between us. If I pursue them, and they turn back to close the gap and grasp my hands, what will I do?

The Amish and Mennonite settlers in Pennsylvania treasured the stories as I do. The Mennonites in Ephrata somehow found the resources to print a full German translation of the original Dutch. Printing started in 1748. When complete, the tome of more than 1500 pages measured 15 by 10 by 5 inches, at that time the largest book printed in Colonial America. It's likely that our Hostetler ancestors in Berks County, Pennsylvania, saw the book or heard the stories before the Indian raid of 1757. Perhaps the histories of van Braght's Defenseless Christians strengthened Jacob's decision to not defend his family against their attackers.

I returned to their story, curious about Jacob Hostetler's unfortunate wife, whom William F. Hochstetler suggests was named Anna Lorentz. It's not clear whether she was born in the Amish community or married into it, but she agreed to sail with Jacob on the *Harle*. Perhaps they sought to put a greater distance between themselves and the threat of torture, or perhaps they were inspired by the feats of their ancestors to seek new hardships.

In the story, the peaches are ripe: autumn. The family hosted an apple schnitzing at their home. Anna may have been a jolly woman, glad to host the community young folk, or she may have just wanted help slicing her apples. What I do know is that after everyone went home, late at night, a party of Delaware Indians arrived. They had no interest in apple schnitzing.

The Delaware hoped to harry settlers off land that had once been theirs. They came at night in small parties to the fringes of settlements, killing or capturing the inhabitants of one house and leaving the neighbors alone, slipping away before sunrise. Our family stories generally ignore the fact that three French scouts joined in the raid on the Hostetler family.

The Hostetlers barricaded themselves in the house. The oldest boys reached for their hunting rifles, but Jacob commanded them to put down the guns. I try to imagine Anna Lorentz that night. Did she approve, fold her hands in her lap, and trust God? Did she remember the martyrs' witnesses and give her husband a gimlet eye to remind him of his faith? Or did she plead with him to use the guns? Was the refusal to bear arms a shared decision or his first display of authority after years of following orders?

When the Delaware set the house afire, the family fled to the cellar, hoping to last until dawn. With barrels of apple cider they quenched the sparks that fell among them, but they feared for their lives. At sunrise the attackers dispersed. But one Delaware lingered behind to gather peaches. He saw the family slipping out the cellar window and called his companions back. There was no need to hurry. Anna, a woman of considerable girth, had stuck fast in the window, and the family stopped to help. I don't know whether they got her out of the window or if the Indians stabbed her as she struggled there. She died by the knife.

William F. Hochstetler says that murder by knife wasn't viewed as an honorable death by the Indians, and it suggests a particular grudge against Anna; she may have had earlier contact with her attackers. One story attempts to explain the raid:

years before the massacre, she'd turned away a party of Indians who came begging at her door. Jason shook his head over this—it was less verifiable than the other facts, he said, which appear in various letters and news accounts of the time. And even if Anna had turned away someone, I saw no direct link to the attack. We might as well say they stabbed her because she scolded the attackers, harangued the one who lingered to steal peaches. Maybe Anna liked peaches. It could have been her own tree, planted with the pit of a peach brought from the Lorentz homestead in the old world where she was born.

But the knife story wasn't the only hint that my ancestress was not a pleasant woman. Hochstetler records a Michael Hostetler who immigrated with the Hostetlers but turned back. A single line suggests that he was Jacob's brother, and that he left because of the way Anna treated him. What if this woman I was trying to claim as a family martyr was actually a bitch? What about the other martyrs far back in history: were they the outspoken ones, the obstinate ones, the ones with too much temper to lay low? *The Martyrs Mirror* contains the letters that Maeyken Wens, she of the tongue screw, sent to her husband, a local mason and an Anabaptist pastor. Why was she was imprisoned and burned, while he escaped censure? Are we surviving Anabaptists calm and quiet as a result of unnatural selection?

There's a final tradition about Anna. Months later, Jacob escaped and wandered for days, certain that had lost his way. Hopeless and starving, he stumbled on the maggoty remains of a possum and ate, ravenously. He fell asleep, and in his dreams Anna appeared, telling him he was going in the right direction. Did he dream her young and supple or wreathed in blood and flame, or both? Did she speak as a saint or an angel, or was it a tongue-lashing?—"Get up, you fool, press on!"

Jason caught me up on his latest reading. According to Virgil Miller,[4] Jacob's wife has been mistakenly named. A Moravian Hostetler immigrant, not our Amish Hostetler, sailed on the *Harle* in 1736 and married a woman named Anna Lorentz. Our Jacob actually sailed in 1738 on the *Charming Nancy*, married to a woman who was probably named Anna. The family record is corrupt: no one remembers Jacob's wife's name. For my ancestress, there is no Lorentz peach orchard to dream of, gazing East. She has no family name at all. On the plus side, the mistreated brother-in-law goes with the Moravian crew. Maybe my ancestress wasn't so bad after all, or maybe her reputation tainted Anna Lorentz' story. In the end, all I could say for certain is that she died horribly.

The more I heard, the more empty-handed I felt. This new book lists her as Anna Burki, question mark. Anna the hostess: round and apple-cheeked; overtaken by events, she dies tragically and returns, an angel, in a dream. Or Anna, sharp-tongued devotee of the way of peace: unsparing of opinions to family and strangers, urging them to sit down and say grace before she hands out peach fritters, dying as she must, a sarcastic saint. Or Anna the harridan: frustrated, bitter, fat on sorrow. She didn't know when she married this Amish man that he would prefer the terrors of the frontier to the religious prejudice of her homeland, that he would ask her to plunder their stores for anyone who asked, to give up her safety for a dream of peace in a hard new land.

And then, learning more history, I found that the very name Anabaptist was questionable, that the word means *re-baptizer* and was abhorrent to my forebears. They didn't consider themselves rebaptized—it was their first baptism, infant baptism didn't count. They had no wish to be executed as Anabaptists, but they kept arguing the point. Pages of the *Martyrs Mirror* are devoted to the court arguments of my righteous, contentious predecessors. The authorities were generally unconvinced. All that blood and fire, for a technicality.

Who are we, then? The Mennonites and Amish broke themselves into dozens of subgroups and conferences with different names, all over fine points. Pick a name, any name: Old Order Amish, Conservative Mennonite, Swartzentruber Amish, Evangelical Mennonite Church, Mennonite Brethren, Old German Baptist Brethren, Mennonite Church USA, Beachy Amish Mennonite. And that's just a sample from the United States. I won't venture into Canada, let alone the rest of the world—and there are more of us outside than inside North America. Van Braght calls us simply Christians, or the brethren, which is problematic today, as an associated group, the Dunkards, still goes by the name Brethren. Brethren is a problem for me, anyway, because I am a woman—what of Ursel, Maeyken Wens, my no-name ancestress, and all the others?

Thieleman J. van Braght may have forgiven his enemies, but he kept good records of his people's wrongs, down to the last confiscated guilder. Did he write *Mirror* so the martyrs' children and great-grandchildren might also have the opportunity to forgive? Or to remind those of us in quieter generations that our piety lacks proof? Jason and I aren't the only ones who have welcomed this dubious reminder over the years—more than three centuries past its first publication, the book is still in print. Ours is the twenty-fourth printing of the second English edition.

In North America today, we descendants of the early Anabaptists are free to baptize any way we wish. We can refuse war, become conscientious objectors, by filling out a form. We tend to get richer than makes us comfortable, because we believe in good work. We try to compensate for our easy lives with personal sacrifice, go out of our way to seek hardship. Mennonite historian Al Keim once told me the story of an Amish farmer who made a fortune on grain during the second world war. The man was so distressed by the weight of his money that he gave it all away to a Mennonite relief organization, to be free of it as quickly as possible.

Others of us quiet our consciences by collecting school supplies to send to children in third world countries, sending work teams to hurricane-flattened neighborhoods, raising our children overseas where we hand out canned meat to refugees. Some devote themselves to taking care of the earth: they pay self-imposed gasoline taxes, put in long hours to starting food cooperatives, and farm vegetables organically. I'd wager that more Mennonites have a copy of the *More With Less* or *Simply in Season* cookbooks, which emphasize health, thrift, and sustainability, than possess the *Martyrs Mirror*.

For all of my sheltered childhood, I am still a product of this time, this culture, my liberal arts education. There are few churches that I can enter without leaving parts of myself outside. But I love the four-part hymns I grew up singing and I believe in the way of peace. What of my spiritual ancestors, the ones in tongue screws, the ones hung in cages, the ones stretched on the rack because they couldn't stop talking about it? Should I be ashamed of their fanaticism, or should I be ashamed of my own small faith? In the shadow of their fiery acts of renunciation, my ambitions for good seem small and dim, my beliefs wavering and insufficient. And yet I nourish them.

Even at a Mennonite college, it was difficult to be completely myself: I found friends among the artsy types who couldn't care less about the martyrs, the activists who saw faith as an obstacle to freedom, and the wholesome, bread baking folk who might have been troubled by my lack of biblical literalism. I hid pieces of myself. I found comrades and mentors to nourish the different pieces of my soul, but few could be part of all my worlds. It's an old story: I was lonely.

There's a story about loneliness that's also a story about the Hostetler name. You might hear it in Switzerland, if you asked an old-timer. In the mid-fourteenth century, plague decimated the villages of Europe and wiped out two hamlets in the region of Schwarzenburg. The ghost villages Aekenmatt and Hostetten stood close together, but a deep ravine and rushing stream separated their dead. If you were the young woman standing at the edge on the Aekenmatt side, you would have seen one light shining in one house on the other side. And when the last man left in Hostetten looked across and saw your single lantern, he would have known he wasn't quite alone, yet. He crosses the ravine, clasps your hand, and you bury your dead. Where you go, you become known as the family from Hostetten, the Hostetlers.

When Jason found his way to my heart, with his willingness to join me in the lonely regions of life, I felt my light doubled. Here was a farm boy immersed in technology, equally excited by genealogy and string theory, who grew up loving Jesus and wary of church authority, who argues the way of peace and chose his own baptism as a child, who feels the call of the land and a simple life, yet longs to be engaged in the world of the mind. I felt complete.

For our first anniversary, Jason and I skipped the romantic

weekend getaway and bought a water buffalo through Heifer Project, an organization (started by a Mennonite) which distributes animals and training to those in need. I feel the glare of Thieleman J. van Braght upon my back. "Is that all?" he asks, "Is that the best you can give? A water buffalo? While you sit home in comfort!"

We arrived at my parents' for Christmas to find my father's present for us: another water buffalo. He shares our ancestors, after all. It is through him I first heard the stories, inherited the sense of obligation. How big must the herd be, how empty our pockets, our houses, how much flesh must we flay from our bones before we feel we've expiated the ease of our lives?

One day, sifting through the *Martyrs Mirror,* I found a tiny souvenir. It was a tenuous connection, like all these links I try to make with history, but the name fit. I found it in a list appended to the German edition of the *Martyrs Mirror*, published in Ephrata before the French and Indian war. It was a list of martyrs from the Tower Book of Berne. On the 28th of May, 1538, two women were executed for their faith. One, I read, was a woman from Hoestetten. Jason taught me how to run my finger lightly across a printed page and feel the ink of the letters, and I did it then. The word stood up in barely perceptible relief from the page: Hoestetten. It was an object in its own right, separate from the paper, placed on this page of copy after copy of this book by generations of people who didn't want me to forget. I could almost scoop it up, almost hold it in my hand.

5

Milk

Brunswick County, Virginia

I've taken possession of the farm kitchen to toss a taco salad and buzz up berry smoothies while Harold and Elaine finish the evening chores. In this yellow-curtained kitchen, Elaine washes the dishes after every meal so there's plenty of counter space. In our own little kitchen where we now house-sit in Harrisonburg, Virginia, I let the dishes pile up while I spend my days studying and writing. I come by this honestly—my mother sometimes let the dishes collect for several days, back before my sister and I were old enough for dish duty.

Elaine, though, was a home economics major. She takes pride in a weed-free garden and well-ironed shirts and worries if there isn't time to vacuum before company comes, even if it's just us. She knows instinctively, or through careful study, what to wear and what to serve. When Harold married her, they warned him not to cleave to a woman with more education than he had, but he ignored the warning. With Elaine's farm upbringing and the college polishing, she can do all things necessary on the homestead—with panache. He's never gone a day hungry.

Whenever we visit the farm, I enjoy puttering around with the extra ovens and the contents of two well-stocked freezers. Cooking is my usual contribution—my mom taught me how to bake bread—but I don't know anything about farm work. This time, when the Alderfers finally come in for supper, I tell Elaine that I'll milk with her in the morning if she'll let me. It's time to learn what the dairy's about.

"But you'll need clothes," she says. I brought old clothes along. A bandanna, too. I'm prepared. I ask when she starts.

"You don't need to come out until five or so."

"But when do *you* start?"

She starts at four. I set my alarm for 4:01. Bring on the camera crews: Does She Have What it Takes to be a Farmwife?

At 4:01, there's not even a hint of grey in the sky. I leave Jason sleeping, fumble into the old pants and T-shirt I laid out last night, and feel my way downstairs. In the kitchen, I drink a quick glass of milk, wondering whether it will be the last one I can stomach for a while.

Across the driveway, light pours from the milkroom door. Elaine already has ten cows lined up in the parlor. She works her way down the line, cleaning udders and spraying them with iodine. I follow, wiping the teats with clean rags, tossing the dirty rags into a quickly filling laundry basket. Barrels of water go into making this milk. We hose down the parlor constantly, every time a cow relieves itself in great, oatmealy plops. We spray down the milkers whenever the cows kick them off. When we finish, we'll run super-heated water through the machines and rinse down the whole parlor. The cows themselves each drink fifty gallons a day.

I wipe down the cows, amazed that they let a stranger approach their udders for introduction. I'm impressed, too, by the variety. Some of these cows milk only in three quarters, the fourth teat hanging high and dry. Some have four teats close together, pointing primly down; other teats point in the four ordinal directions from a ballooning bag. Some cows milk best from their rear quarters, so Elaine has to remove the milkers from the two high front teats to let the sagging hind ones milk out. She walks down the rows of machines, testing udders, knowing by some alchemy which are finished milking and which are still full.

Any woman who worries about the width, the breadth, the volume, or the evenness of her bust should spend a morning with these creatures. She should examine these bare udders, note where Elaine singed the hair away so deftly that the cows didn't flinch. She should take a good look at their tit-warts and contemplate the surprising number of cows who have a fifth, vestigial teat hanging barnacle-like to the side of the udder.

* * *

I don't make a practice of worrying about the breadth of my bosom, and for this I thank my own mother. Mom made it clear that our worth had nothing to do with our looks. She didn't quote Proverbs at us (*Beauty is fleeting and charm is deceptive*—we got that from the Christian teen magazines), but she lived outside of the transactions of fashion herself. She was no plain Mennonite; she gave up her Sunday head covering along with most of her peers in the bell-bottom years. She had two tubes of lipstick and a bottle of foundation that never emptied until my sister and I co-opted it for our teenage experiments. Sometimes she curled her hair for church. That was the extent of her primping. She didn't dissuade us from our forays into makeup and ear piercing, but it was quite clear that we were on our own.

She didn't teach us about hair removal either; perhaps she didn't want to pressure us into premature womanhood. I endured hairy-legged junior high gym classes for months before I summoned the courage to ask Mom for a razor, blushing furiously. My sister took charge of her own fashion training, researching how to pouf her bangs and the right way to roll her sleeves and peg her jeans, and she showed me how I ought to do it, too. She spent her small clothing budget on hairspray and items that would help her blend in at our public high school.

In time, to be different, I began to raid the vintage stores. I appalled my sister with my cloche hats, argyle socks pulled up to my knees, tattered skirts, and jingly silver belts. To my great satisfaction, she'd say, "You're wearing *that?*"

Mom made no comment on our fashion choices, but she let me plunder her closet for her old clothes.

* * *

I'm glad I brought old clothes as I dodge the latest spout of steaming shit. I reach again for the hose. Elaine presses a button on each milker when the cow has almost milked out, and the machine gradually surrenders its suction and retracts on its cable, hanging behind the cow like a plastic octopus. As tired as she must be from staying up to talk last night, Elaine moves efficiently from cow to cow, intuiting when they're finished.

She comes from a line of hard-working Mennonite farm women. She grew up on a farm in Minnesota, remembers using an outhouse and the arrival of electricity. They milked the cows into buckets, with primitive versions of these machines. She wore a prayer doily to church for most of her life—Jason remembers her pinning it on. Now, with no Mennonites in this part of the country, she wears elegant ensembles with well-matched accessories to the local Baptist church.

I follow the line again, dipping each teat in antibiotic solution. The tit-dip drips and stains my arms yellow until I learn to dip the front teats first. The cow's quarters, now empty of milk, deflate against each other, crossing like fingers, making it difficult to dip them individually. The cows don't help either. I have to dodge the pendulums of their manure-laden tails. It's real physical work, a change from my sedentary student lifestyle, reading stories, writing them.

* * *

Mom used to read to us in the evenings and tell folktales while we weeded the flowerbeds. My parents saw no need for television, so we learned narrative from Mom. Meanwhile, we missed out on mainstream images of women. We were glad Cinderella ended up with her prince, but we knew that her success had everything to do with her own bravery and cleverness—and the skills of her godmother. That's how Mom told the story: without mice. I remember her grudging acceptance when my sister entered the Indian Summer Queen Pageant, complete with evening gown competition. Mom was more impressed when we won awards in science fairs or acted in school plays.

She was a "stay-at-home" mom. She took good care of us but made us participate in that care. We all cleaned house on the weekends, crossing jobs off a master list. We girls washed the dishes. We were to tear ourselves away from our summer reading to help weed the garden and put up produce, but Mom didn't value hard work for itself. It was a means to an end. Work was to be finished quickly so you could putter over your flowers, write letters and poems, or read a novel, sprawled on the living room floor with a snack, preferably chocolate, at your elbow.

She spent her time in ways that made no sense economically. Some mornings, she'd sit by the windows for an hour or more, lost in her prayers or daydreams, the stack of notecards with prayer requests held loosely in her hands, its rubber band lost. She preferred working outside: cutting paths through the woods, concocting strategies to keep the deer out of the orchard. She volunteered at the elementary school and the library. A few times, when she had to, she worked part time in town. She didn't ever seem to be trying to get ahead, to get anywhere. She enjoyed some things, and cried over others. She could be socially awkward or a super host, depending on her mood and the situation.

I worried about her when I left home. What would she do? I urged her to pick up where she'd left off with the novel in her bottom drawer, a book she'd abandoned twenty years before. She did. Now she writes, spinning the novel into a series. Perhaps she would have done it without my urging. Perhaps she would have sat a little longer each morning, forgetting the world.

My mother was no minivan mom. She wasn't obsessed with our appearance or our success. She didn't drive us to our school events, she didn't encourage us to sign up for them, she didn't ask us about our homework, she didn't box up nutritious lunches for us. We walked to school, packed our own lunches, made A's, took too many extracurriculars. She didn't force a particular way of being a woman upon us. She let us find our own ways.

* * *

I have to find a way to get the next batch of cows into the parlor. We open the gate to let this bunch out, huge beasts who could just as easily wander down onto the parlor floor as out the door and down the ramp to the barn. But they go where they should, kept moving more by the pushing of the cows behind them than by my feeble, "Go on!" Their hips are so wide that the largest must pull them between the wall and the stanchions as she goes along—five little tugs to get to the end of the parlor.

Elaine closes the gate behind them. I'm supposed to go out in the alley and bring in another ten cows. One or two, with their noses already poking into the parlor, come in as soon as I open the door, but the rest stay outside. They turn their backs on me, ignore the tapping of my stick.

Elaine comes out to help, and with a loud "Here cow, here cow," she soon has one singled out and swatted into place.

"Just don't let them come up behind you, or you'll get squished between them," she warns. After a while, I learn to approach each cow briskly, confidently, with a clear idea of what I want them to do. Like children directed by a confident adult, they obey, mostly. One cow refuses to be milked on the left-hand side of the parlor and has to be driven through the right-hand door. Another one, barely more than a heifer, hangs back until the end. She dreads the oxytocin shot we have to give her because she hasn't learned to let her milk down. She'll figure it out eventually, Elaine assures me.

***

We sometimes resented being left alone to figure out womanhood for ourselves. We wanted someone to tell us what to wear, how to act around boys, how to be ladylike. We wanted someone to clear up the question of whether we should plan to be mothers or plan to be PhD's, or both. Mom didn't seem to care either way. It was all very well for her to wear blue jeans and run around in the woods and love stories and pray and bake bread, but how were we supposed to get on in the real world?

I still haven't figured that out. I'm not cut out for either style of housewifery, the dreamy earthchild or the indomitable pioneer. This is the dilemma for my generation of Mennonite women: Martha could knead the bread and Mary could watch it rise, but we feel we should earn our bread, maximize our career potentials, justify our educations. I long to avoid the questions of jobs and money and nylons, and I fear the demands of motherhood. I'm still learning how to nourish even myself.

For the rest of our visit, I will help with morning milking and marvel at how weak I am compared to Elaine. I'll collapse into longer and longer naps in the heat of the afternoon. Being a farm wife calls on strength that is foreign to me. I'll chart my possible courses: Teaching? An artistic career? Bread-baking? Milking cows?

Martyrs and Chickens

This is the gift that my mother gave me: a door, wide open.

* * *

We milk about eighty cows before we're done. I open the gate wide to let the last ones out. Their faces are delicate, the bone structure plainly visible through their soft leather skins, their eyes large and sensitive. They step like dancers, careful not to slip on the wet floor. I feel an impulse to thank them for the morning, for the milk, for the complicated relationship we have.

I clean and hang the tentacled milkers on their hooks, then hose down the parlor. The black sky has turned to gray by the time I finish. The banty rooster crows his first morning crow, and I stumble inside for a little more sleep.

6

Amish Country

Holmes County, Ohio

The man behind the bullet-proof glass in the hotel lobby asks if we've ever been to Holmes and Tuscarawas counties before. We shake our heads. He decides that the boy in the flannel shirt and the girl in frayed Indian-print pants are harmless and pushes open his office door to bring us tourist pamphlets. Women wearing prayer coverings beam up from the glossy brochures, and men in straw hats and untamed beards carve wood. The wineries all have buggies in their logos. The clerk assumes that we're here to goggle at the Amish, but we are Amish, practically. Half-Amish. Jason and I figured it up by counting our great-great-grandparents: adding our bloodlines together, you get 17/16ths of an Amish person and 15/16ths of a Mennonite.

We're here on family business. We want to visit the historical society and ferret out information on a legendary relative, Jonas Stutzman, who dressed in white from his hat to his shoes. Jason is also tracking his great-great-grandmother's first husband, who died in a boiler explosion. And we might swing by Lehman's non-electric store, the mecca of homesteaders, the store that made a Y2K fortune when folks stuffed their garages full of generators and lanterns and fireplace popcorn poppers.

In the morning, we find our breakfast at one of the enormous feeding-houses built along Route 39. We're sad to see they don't serve scrapple,[5] but our waitresses wear pinafores, and racks of Amish books, Amish soft drinks, and Amish toys block the way to the cash register. As we exit, a group of Amishmen enters. I avert my eyes, trying to neutralize the overdose of stares they must receive daily, trying to send out Mennonite vibes: *I'm sort of like you, even though I drive a car and watch cable television. Sort of. I believe in peace, too, and simple living. I've milked a cow. With help.*

You can tell the moment that Route 39 enters Holmes County because the brittle, tar-patched road evens out into a smooth ride for tourists, and every fifty feet another sign promotes Heini's cheese factory. We turn up Route 77 and stop at the Mennonite and Amish heritage center, Behalt.

Milton Yoder, in the dark, collarless coat of a conservative Mennonite, guides us though the central attraction of Behalt, the cyclorama. The mural encircles an enormous round room with overlapping scenes rendered in Heinz Gaugel's vibrant—some might say garish—hues. Yoder uses a laser pointer to indicate important events in Anabaptist history.

First, of course, comes Christ, muscular and oddly golden at his crucifixion. After him come scenes of early martyrs and their persecution by the institutionalized church, the rebaptized heroes Grebel, Blaurock, and Manz. We contemplate a headless neck, cartoonish with the white end of the bone visible, the cut flesh red around it like a ribeye steak. Ulrich Ulman, the first Anabaptist beheaded.

"It's a bit exaggerated," explains Yoder. He turns our attention quickly to the elusive Menno Simons, slipping away to safety on a blue night with his wife and child. Later comes a house on fire, the Hostetlers in Berks County, Pennsylvania, getting slaughtered in a raid during the French and Indian War.

"Our ancestors!" we say excitedly. "We know that story."

Yoder nods. "There are lots of you."

Finally we reach the man we've been watching for—Jonas Stutzman in white coat and pants, gazing up into the sky in feverish anticipation, his white beard wild in hurricane-strength winds, his hands uplifting a chair to the heavens. Because of the overlapping perspectives of the mural, Jonas Stutzman looks to be standing on the backs of two shaggy oxen. It suits him.

Yoder explains that Jonas Stutzman believed Jesus would return in 1853 and set up office in Holmes County, so he built a chair for him. The seat was six inches higher than normal "because Christ should be above everyone else." He turns us around so that we can see what was hidden by the central pillar when we entered the room. The chair that Jonas built sits on a little pedestal. It's roughly hewn of a wood I can't name, the seat woven with strips of cane. Jonas is long gone, but the chair still waits for Jesus.

A final set of scenes shows Anabaptist congregations worshiping: an Amish church, Hutterite and Conservative Mennonite congregations, and Conference Mennonites, with men and women sitting together. I am what they call here a conference Mennonite, but I don't wear a small prayer covering on my head like the long-haired women on the wall. In the gift shop, I have a chance to try on a larger net covering, but don't take it. My mother and grandmother removed theirs years ago, and I'm not eager to go back. Instead, we plunder the bookstore for genealogical materials. In the booklet *Some Fascinating Stutzman Ancestors*, Greg Hartzler-Miller tells about two of Jonas Stutzman's brothers: Jost went into the Pennsylvania House of Representatives, Christian to the Ohio Lunatic Asylum.

Before we go, we sign the guest register. "Oh!" says the woman who watches the desk, a Conservative Mennonite, I guess, from her head covering and sensible shoes. "You're a Beachy? So was I." I'm glad I kept my name when I married Jason. It's nice to have something to link me to this community where family and faith and memory run together, even though my clothing makes me incognito, even though the act of keeping my name separates me, too. The conservative woman gives us directions to an Amish library and suggests we stop at the lumber company for help.

Back on the road, we're surprised by how much congestion the buggies cause, then realize that all the cars are the real problem. It's not that the buggies are too slow—it's that the rest of us are far too fast. How could we forget, when we planned this trip, that it would be Memorial Day weekend? We can't tell which of the unmarked houses on a back road is the library, so we backtrack to the lumber company and Jason disappears inside. I bury my face in a book as Amish folk hurry in and out, afraid they might gawk at me.

Jason returns with the key, and we find the place and let ourselves in. There's no electricity, but gas lights hang from the ceiling and, oddly enough, a copy machine sits in one corner. We search the shelves by the light from the windows. Genealogy, Anabaptist literature, back issues of local papers. Surprises, too: A floor-to-ceiling shelf of National Geographics. Dostoevsky. Turgenev. Along one wall sit two small chairs, just like Jesus' chair at the museum, but kid-sized. The placard says Jonas Stutzman traveled from household to household making chairs without nails, joining green and dry wood together so the fittings would tighten as the wood shrank.

Our second family question resolves when we find, hanging on the wall, the original newspaper article about the 1882 boiler explosion that killed Jason's great-great-grandmother's husband, George Stutzman. The boiler ran a steam-powered sawmill, and four men died when it burst. The article unflinchingly describes how one man was "bursted open and part of his internal organs out" and the "fence rail smeared with blood and flesh." The wooden frame the article hangs in was made from pieces of that fence.

We're hungry for lunch despite the gory account, so we drive down streets of ginger-breaded Amish Treasures and kitschified Amish Kitchens, double-parked, sidewalks choked with holidayers. We break out our emergency pretzels and drive to Kidron, where we find a lunchroom hidden under a grocery store and eat our two-dollar sandwiches surrounded by Amish kids.

Lehman's General Store. If the homesteading movement had a Mecca, this might be it. We've spent the past few years poring over the contraptions in their catalogue: mills we could use to grind our wheat into flour, if we grew our own wheat; churns for butter, if we had a cow; fruit dryers for preserving the harvest of the peach and apple orchards in our minds' eyes. We enter the original part of the store, a reconstructed log house. Warehouses extend the footprint of the store, and a flock of storage barns gathers behind it.

At first I'm skeptical that Amish would actually shop here, eying pricey pottery and even more expensive Amish-made baskets. But then I enter a room full of bells—sleigh bells of all sizes, brass bells from Germany, cow bells, great black dinner bells to hang outside. The Amish might come here to buy bells. There are windchimes, too, enormous ones as resonant as church-bells, like the ones we bought last year at the Mennonite Central Committee Relief Sale, the ones too loud to hang outside in the crowded suburb where we live.

As we venture past the imported tin toys and Amish-made marble rollers, more practical implements appear: walls of rakes, hoes, forks, scythes, spades, a mallet of rolled rawhide, honest purchases, like the jelly jars I think of buying for the strawberries I plan to U-pick next month. We find a copper cauldron big enough to boil me in, a giant wooden spoon to match. If I made jam to fill this pot, it would last for decades—unless we had a dozen children. Looking at the cookstoves, I long, perhaps foolishly, for the retired Alderfer family stove back on Jason's folks' farm, with its shiny enamel, its firebox, the widened margins of error and perfection in bread-baking. I want to know how to use such things.

Such things are all about, hanging from the ceiling, even, to create an old-time ambience: rusty hay rakes and wringer-washers, a funny four-runnered sled. Take a look at the classic Hoosier cabinet with its flour sifter, rollback doors, and spice racks. You could put in a whole set of kitchen cabinets for its price. "We have one of those back home on the farm," says Jason. "We put the mail on it." Move on to the laundry room. Here's an expensive, eco-friendly Staber washer that uses less water and detergent to wash bigger loads with a shorter spin cycle. For the hardcore non-electric Amish, there are galvanized steel laundry tubs with hand wringers attached.

We buy nothing but stagger back out to the car to nap until the next rainstorm passes. When we return to the Amish library, I sleep some more as Jason goes next door to see if the caretaker is home yet. I wake to hear a generator kicking on. So that's how they run the Xerox machine. I pick up the book about Jonas Stutzman. He once broke his leg cutting wood five miles from home, made a splint and crutches, and hobbled home. Later in life, he had his visions of Christ's return, used the "science of numbers" to pin down the date, and wrote five different Appeals to his fellow men and women. There's no indication that Jonas ever had a following inside or outside of the church, but on the other hand, no one ever tried to put him in the Ohio Lunatic Asylum like his brother. I get the sense that people tolerated his visions. He called for support of his ill-conceived cause in his third Appeal:

> All those individuals, who sincerely and seriously desire to take active interest in the great cause of God, are hereby requested, to inform me thereof in post-paid letter, in which they also may advise me somewhat more in detail of the various circumstances of their situation, to enable me thereby to perceive more clearly and judge more correctly—how—where—and in what manner their cooperation may be rendered most available for the promotion of this holy cause. Please direct to: Jonas Stutzman, Walnut Creek Post Office, Holmes County, Ohio.

1853 came and went without Christ's return, but Jonas continued to wear white for the rest of his life. His confidence in "the science of numbers" and his ability to predict the proper time were dashed. A friend discovered Jonas's grandfather clock in the pigsty.

Jason returns from the library victorious, with copies in hand, and we start the long drive home. He tells me the boiler explosion happened because George Stutzman, his almost-ancestor, weighted the escape valve so the boiler would provide more power. The men knew it wasn't safe, but joked that if it blew, only four would be killed and plenty of workers were around to take their places.

I watch the farmsteads pass the window, clean and green from the rain. Sometimes, I think, civilization is like an overweighted boiler. We know it will blow sometime, at least run out or boil over; it's a great pyramid scheme that doesn't account for the reality of limited natural resources. Sometimes I think I should go home to the Amish, beg them to take me in now, before the refugees come streaming over the hills from the cities.

It's not that I want to be Amish, to wear long sleeves on summer days and submit to one rigid version of goodness—years from now, I will see with even more clarity what it could mean to be a woman or dreamer or dissident of any sort in a conformist sect, and when I see a young girl in plainclothes in a restaurant, my first impulse will not be to compare genealogies but, instead, to slip her my card and tell her to call if she ever needs a ride out of there.

Nevertheless, I want to step outside the economy of useless possessions, work that uses only a small fraction of my capabilities as a human creature. I'm soft, easily tired. My muscles don't know what it is to work, barely remember the joy in the power of stacking wood with my dad. I want a piece of land, a garden, wheat fields, chickens. I want a windmill and solar panels. I want to kill the meat I eat. But I'd still like to write, to make phone calls, to read shocking novels, to go to the theater. I want to join the young green wood of my life to old wood, to build something sturdy, something that holds up over time.

"Wouldn't it be neat," I ask Jason, "To live off the grid? We could run a Staber washer with solar power and bake with the family wood oven."

"Seems like an expensive hobby," he says, even though he agrees.

We pass a silo with an advertisement painted on it—a bear stealing away with a roll of carpeting in its paws: Bear Country Floor Coverings. Bear Country. We've left Amish Country behind.

It's nuts to even think of giving up our indoor jobs, inexpensive commodities, the energy of the thundering heavens straight from Dominion Power, for a monthly fee. We'd need a community to support us, a remote location to protect us from gawkers, vision. We'd need to find people who don't mind wearing white shoes after Labor Day, who wanted to build something for Jesus, something nobody's built yet, a divine toothpick in preparation for the day when he stops in for dinner on his stroll around the kingdom of Heaven, which, as he said, is here.

In the spirit of Jonas Stutzman, I appeal to all those individuals, who sincerely and seriously desire to take active interest in this great cause of God: please inform me thereof via email, and advise me how, where, and in what manner your cooperation may be rendered most available for the promotion of this holy cause. Please direct them to me, Subject: Neo-Amish Utopia.

7
Selling the Farm

Brunswick County, Virginia

Friday

In the back seat of the Corolla, the chickens hyperventilate, their gasping clucks accusing us through the holes punched in their cardboard boxes. There's not much we can do. It's the middle of the night and we're caught in a traffic jam on Interstate 64. The exhaust fumes and diesel motors growling on and off bother us, too, but our pampered backyard chickens are convinced that this is the end, that they will die here on the interstate. Jason and I loosen the tops of their boxes, but there's not much we can do until we've crept the two miles to the spot where the Jaws of Life and emergency vehicles gather, where road crews sweep up the broken glass of someone's disaster.

We acquired the chickens last fall. We're finally renting a place with enough room for creatures and a few weedy tomatoes. We're taking the chickens with us to the farm because we plan to stay for an entire week, help Jason's parents prepare for Wednesday's auction, then stay to watch the cows and equipment go. Last August, Harold started talking about giving up the dairy business and going to work for a John Deere dealer. We guessed it would still be years before the folks moved.

But at Christmas, family rumor had it they'd be selling soon. The noisy Alderfer get-together might be the last one on the farm, implied the noisy Alderfers. Jason and I brushed off their remarks. But the decision came quickly, by February. We maxed out our long-distance calling minutes that month for the first time, talking to family. Milk prices were down, gas prices were up. The farm debts weren't getting any smaller. It was hard to get good help, and Elaine and Harold were working too hard. We feared for their health. Jason's stomach wasn't right, and neither was his sleep.

In March, when we last visited, Harold's stomach wasn't good either. We arrived late at night to find him, as usual, in the armchair waiting to go check the cows a final time. He didn't even greet us, just looked up out of the chair with eyes that glittered in the dark. He'd been prostrate from food poisoning all week, in between farm work, flat on his back. Elaine wondered whether the stomach trouble could come from deciding to sell the farm—a true gut reaction. Maybe the stress weakened his immune system, and bad chicken nuggets did the rest.

By now, April, we're almost used to the idea of selling the farm. We escape from the interstate at the first exit and find a gas station. We buy water in a bottle and pour it into the bottom half of a Styrofoam cup for the chickens to drink. I beg their forgiveness, and three hens graciously grant it, but Miranda turns away, refusing to drink or be comforted.

Saturday Evening

The clocks turn forward tonight. Eight becomes nine, far past Elaine's bedtime. Jason and I take a walk after supper, clouds and a crescent moon above us. We turn on the barn lights so we can see our way. The road by the silo, often deep in mud, is so dry now I can walk it almost blind in my good sandals. I remind Jason that this is a day we've foreseen, ever since that first walk we took on the farm at night, when life together grew into possibility, when I guessed that he would be the one for me, and knew, too, that he wouldn't return to this farm, though parts of him longed to. "But it happened so fast," I say, "Marrying you, and then this. Faster than I imagined."

"That's how it will be at the end of our lives," says Jason. "*It happened so fast.*"

We walk beyond the barns on the drought-packed road. The farm is oriented truly; we're going straight out toward the North Star. He says, "If we weren't selling, it would be bad. They'd have to keep buying feed, and it looks like the wheat won't amount to anything if it doesn't rain." There's not even dew on the wheat tonight.

We sit out in the field, looking back at the farm. Jason observes that silos look taller at night. The world stands starkly in black and gray, like an engraving, the black shapes of the barn and house, the tree line, all small against a sky pricked with white points of light. I lie back in the wheat; it wreaths the stars. Jason points to Spica, Arcturus, Corvus, the crow. I know the story of Orion as my mother told it, how he shot the great bull, Taurus, and saved the seven sisters, but I can only identify Orion. There are no road sounds out here, only frogs and insects. Three different choirs make tonight's cantata—peeping, scraping, and chirring.

We walk back toward the house on the dark side of the silo, to save our night-accustomed eyes. By the old peacock pen, we stop to check on our chickens. By this morning, they'd recovered from the trip, wildly busy with the rampant vetch and chickweed. I sat with them awhile, watching them peck, and thought how strange that these birds would trust me, run to me when I open the door of the pen. I might eat them, after all. "Chick-chick-chick?" I call softly. Someone whines back at me from the shelter of the lean-to we made out of plywood. *Let us sleep.*

We tiptoe past the trailer where Aunt Lorraine has made her home. Jason used to set up his telescope on her back porch, and she'd come out to look at Venus. Past the house, lines of equipment are set up for sale in the front field. The folded row markers of the corn planters rear up against the sky like the heads of midnight brontosauri. The machines sleep, waiting.

Last month we came out here on the lawn-height wheat, where Harold was starting to line up equipment for the sale. Some of the pieces were caked with rust, others still enameled John Deere green. Jason taught me the difference between a V-ripper and a subsoiler, explained the elegances of a circular hay rake and the miracle of a rotary cultivator. I've imagined such machines as impossibly complicated, but seen up close they're intelligent, simple. The row crop cultivator requires that you steer perfectly straight between the rows, but the rotary hoe capitalizes on corn's deep roots, and its gnashing gears spare the crop while laying waste to weeds.

Today, I wrestled roses and pruned butterfly bushes, tore out weeds and honeysuckle, made sloppy Joes for lunch, then salmon loaf, peas, and mashed potatoes for supper; meanwhile, the men unloaded a sod drill, on consignment from another seller for the auction. It took three front-end loaders to lift it up while the truck drove out from under it. Jason took lots of pictures, impressed with weight, and with power.

Sunday

Sundays on the farm are for rest. Sometimes, this means skipping church. Last time, Elaine had nursery duty and Harold had been instructed to stay home because he'd sleep wherever he was and might as well do it in comfort—and because Elaine wouldn't be in the pew beside him to stick an elbow in his ribs whenever the snores got loud. We stayed home, too, drove the pickup out to the back field and tramped back the logging roads behind the woods. It was warm enough to take off my jacket when we climbed uphill, the woods thick with holly, the sky pure blue. Canada geese rubber-necked at us from the pasture pond as we walked back.

Today, too, I stay in all morning, read a novel, go to Pino's for a pizza lunch with the family. At Pino's, Tony, the Guatemalan man who runs this Italian restaurant, says he's thinking of selling out, too. So much stress to keep the place going. "Maybe you will share the money from the sale? With me?" he asks Elaine, his eyes laughing.

Sometimes when I visit, I busy myself all day: baking bread, hauling firewood, getting groceries, cooking meals, washing dishes. Elaine does these sorts of things routinely, plus feeding the calves and milking every morning. What a rest she will have when they're gone. I can't wrap my mind around how it must be to force yourself up at three thirty in the morning and plunge through the rest of the day a task at a time, never resting because each next thing must be done, because without it, someone or something won't be able to eat or have clean clothes, or its udder will burst. I grow weary by late afternoon and drop off the moment I sit in the armchair.

In March, we freed the calves from their hutches. They stood ankle-deep in a mixture of sawdust and manure in small individual stalls. We all helped to move them, one at a time, out to pasture. I filled the syringe for their vaccinations, Jason dug out the muck to open the hutch doors, Elaine held their heads, and Harold gave the injections. Then we led each balky calf down to the field, where, for the first time in their few months of life, they were free to run and eat green grass. They didn't know what to do with their legs but soon set off in a stumbling run, shambling around, meeting the electric fence, kicking up their heels, getting spooked by each other. One of the calves had a white question mark blazoned on its black face, an emblem of all our uncertainty.

I wonder this Sunday, this day of rest, where Harold and Elaine will be this autumn, what they'll be doing, how they'll feel when they've finally caught up on sleep. Will they kick up their heels with freedom?

In the afternoon, Jason finds the body of the last bantam rooster perched in the magnolia. Some stray dogs rampaged through the farm last week and tore off his proud tail. Shortly afterward, he disappeared. Elaine thought the dogs returned and finished him off, but he'd been here all along, clinging to his old roost. Perhaps he died of wounded pride. Elaine is sad to see the rooster go. She gladly made broth from the rest of the flock of bantams and guinea fowl, who scratched up her flowerbeds obsessively, the roosters trumpeting at all hours. "But that last one, he grew on me," she says. Only two are left now, a banty hen and a guinea who roost at night in the magnolia beside his corpse, ever faithful. In a few more weeks, the hen will disappear, and the guinea will spend its days beside its own reflection in the chrome bumper of the Buick.

Monday

Trucks drive in all day, scoping out the sales. A load of heifers to be sold on consignment shows up early. A quartet of auction crewmen look the place over, strategizing. One of Harold's buddies hooked him up with the auctioneer, who's supposed to have connections all over. He has sent fliers for this sale into half a dozen states.

Aunt Loretta drives down from Richmond to help. We let our chickens out of the peacock pen to scratch in the super-sized compost heap. The guinea and banty are curious, but keep their distance. We find a tiny turtle in the window well. "It will snap your finger off," says Jason, but I know better. It's barely the size of my hand, a baby painted turtle, I think, and I reach into the well and rescue it. In the air, it swims, but when I set it down, it retracts into its shell and regards me suspiciously. When I check later, it has trundled away, its tiny estate on its back.

The wind whips up later, and the evening sky cuts pearly holes through the black clouds that roll up from the west. Thunder rumbles and lightning lances distant clouds, while the whole north-western sky turns pink.

"That's hail," says Harold. "Pop used to say a pink sky means hail." I imagine golf-ball sized hail battering the lined-up equipment to bits, shattering the shrubbery, pinging off the turtle's shell. When the rain and thunder are directly overhead, Loretta gets nervous at Harold's prolonged phone calls and makes him get off the phone. Jason tells us about the time lightning zapped their phone, leaving a black smudge on the wall, incinerating the cord.

The worst of the storm passes to the north. Harold says, "The good Lord done us good." Uncle Norton calls Loretta—power's out in his part of Richmond. By bedtime, the storm is past and all is silent.

Tuesday

Today we wait. We clear up trash outside, kidnap some hissing kittens and cuddle them against their will, watch the blue and white striped tent with its ornate wedding-reception walls and windows rise up around a sawdust ring, watch the men arrange rows of gates into corrals and chutes. Uncle Norton arrives in the afternoon with his cameras, and cousin Twila shows up, too. I make taco salad for supper. Jason spends an hour on the phone with work, as the e-mail server is down.

Later, he takes the deceased rooster out of the tree, carrying it before him cradled in a pitchfork, out toward the pond. When he passes the peacock pen, the chickens cluster by the fence to watch, gabbing. *Look! A rooster! I haven't seen a rooster for months.* Jason flings the rooster over a hedge.

Tonight, they'll bury a cow that keeled over in the pasture.

Yesterday, Jason cleaned up two dead cats with the grain shovel.

We meet the auctioneer, Lewis Harrison. He greets us suavely, and when he finds out Jason works with computers, not cows, he says what so many people say: "All I know how to do is press the button off and on."

I wonder if he speaks out of admiration, or if he's trying to console Jason for his indoor life, or both. Harrison expresses concern about the cattle sale. Cows are down from earlier this spring, and no wonder, with milk prices dropping and subsidies slackening. "The equipment should go well," he assures us. "It's the right color—John Deere green." His cell phone won't stop ringing, and he answers every caller as if they're the most important person he knows—and as if he has all the time in the world.

Even more people cruise by, taking their looks. Tomorrow, says Jason, "They'll swarm all over that equipment like ants on sugar." They were starting to swarm as far back as March, when two young men came over to poke around the equipment, then helped Harold locate and fix the source of a rattle in one of his tractors. Over lunch, Harold explained that one of the boys, a nice young fellow, had it rough—"His mom spent all those years in jail for smacking her husband over the head with a frying pan and killing him. Should have let her off—they say she did the community a service."

Wednesday

I wake before dawn. Jason isn't sleeping either—his digestive system keeps him awake. I tiptoe to the bathroom, and on the other side of the wall I hear another toilet flush. Elaine, too, is awake, even though the cows don't have to be milked until after they're sold this morning—they have to enter the sale ring with fat udders, streaming milk. I return to bed, knowing I won't sleep, watch the sky lighten, Venus fading between the dark branches of the pecan, the birds beginning to sing. Later, the sky blues up, the horizon brightens, and the bedroom turns to full color.

We go downstairs to breakfast. I wrap up in my sweatshirt jacket, go out to check the chickens, and snap a few final pictures. There's no one out yet. The cows sell at nine; it's already seven: shouldn't the buyers be here looking them over? What if they go for paltry prices? The outcome of the auction could mean financial ruin or freedom for the Alderfers, though none of us say it out loud.

Aunt Loretta worries about this and about the milking duties—who will milk all the consignment cows? She keeps these worries to herself, but Uncle Norton has no scruples about sharing: "She told me not to tell that she's worried," he says, and proceeds to enumerate her concerns. "She takes on *everyone's* troubles." But we know, even while he scoffs, he's proud of her conscientiousness. He boasts of the time at the library book sale that she discovered a first edition Alcoholics Anonymous manual for two dollars, and took it to the front and informed the sellers that the book would bring six to eight thousand through a dealer. "How many people," asks Norton, "would do such a thing?"

I decide to climb the Harvestor silo, ninety feet, to take pictures of the farm spread out for sale. Jason always bangs the fill pipe on the silo to make the pigeons fly before he begins to climb, but I'd rather risk pigeon droppings than have that noise. Halfway up, the wind buffets hard enough to freeze the windward side of my face, makes me wonder if I should go on. But I climb above the wind, and stand comfortably inside the rail on the top. There's still enough breeze to blow stray wisps of my hair across the camera's viewfinder. I hold them back with one hand, try to hold the camera steady in the other.

From up here, I can see that half of the woods has been logged, a final harvest of the land before it is sold. Its slopes and ravine lay naked now, contours which were once hidden under the pine and holly. Below, Jason and Norton videotape me, tape the chickens. The folks from Rock United Methodist Church are firing up the cookers for breakfast, the ladies Harold calls the Rockettes unloading the biscuits they spent the early morning hours baking. The white and blue tent spreads near the milking parlor, the temporary corrals built from red gates full of waiting cows.

By nine o'clock, the tent is full of people—buyers, we hope. Lewis Harrison introduces Elaine and Harold, and then the herd: "These are honest cows," he says, "Good honest cows." He brings #13 into the ring first, along with her calf, #13-A, who was born yesterday, too late to receive its own number. The wobbly little heifer goes for five hundred dollars—a good sign. We find out later that Harrison bought the calf himself, to get things rolling. He buys for dealers all over the country. One of Harrison's helpers sings the auctioneer's song—"Five, who'llgivme six, givme six; six who'll givme seven?"—but Harrison does the selling.

Of a young heifer, he says, "She's got her whole career ahead of her—look at that udder potential." An average milker: "Put the groceries to her and she'll milk more for you." A dry cow that can't be milked for months until she calves: "She's safe9'til September." A many-calved cow near the end of her career: "Check out that somatic cell count of zero!" And, ubiquitously, "Look at the wheels on that one!" "Look at her silky udder!" He earnestly calls back the buyers' attention when it wanders: "We're buying cows here"—reminds them that this is a bargain, that "a good cow is worth more than that."

Only toward the end of the cattle auction do I notice that he holds the rope to the show ring gate. He swings it open at the crucial moment when the bidding slows, so that as the cow runs out, the bidders feel it's getting away, and the bids escalate into a strong finish.

Outside, in the milking parlor, Aunt Lorraine grumbles to Aunt Loretta and Jason about the auctioneer's patter. "I don't understand why they have to make that sound. Why can't they just, when the cow comes out, say, 'Here she is. What'll you give?'"

Loretta returns to her worries from earlier in the morning, and Jason tells her that today will be like a road trip. "There might be a traffic jam along the way, but we'll just get on that road and drive."

Jason needs to help someone receive a fax, so I take over, grabbing a pole to guide the cows from the chute along the barn, into the holding pen, and into the parlor. Most, streaming milk, don't need any urging, and I lean on my staff like Bo-Peep until a cow gets interested in sniffing the boxwoods, or the cat and her two kittens inside of them, and needs a little nudge on her way. Newborn #13-A slumbers on the other side of the fence, under the boxwoods, too small to be placed in the triangle of gates that holds the other bottle calves.

More family arrive, just in time to snap a picture of Harold scaling the fence. They make him stop on the top, for their shot, and he grimaces. "That's not as easy as it used to be," he says, safe on the other side. When the cows that used to belong to the Alderfers are milked, we turn the parlor over to the auction crew to milk the consignment cows, and we go inside for hot dogs and sweet potato pie with the relatives. The milk from the foreign cows will go down the drain—we can't risk having our tank contaminated with antibiotics.

In the afternoon, everyone gathers around the chopper, the first equipment piece to be auctioned. The auctioneer pages Harold Alderfer from the loudspeaker on the auction truck, but he's not around. I jog back to the house and find him deep in conversation, as usual, with some friends. And also as usual, it's impossible to tell if they're new friends, or folks that he's known all his life, but I tear him away and we sail down in the four-wheeled Gator. He climbs up into the auction truck, looking a bit uncomfortable, ready to answer questions about the equipment.

Down in the crowd, Lewis Harrison plies his mesmerism, conducting the buyers like an orchestra, sweeping his hands around the circle, cuing the uncertain with an eyebrow, raising his arms sharply, straight up—Sold!

I don't understand much about the equipment sale, except that some things are going for scrap metal prices, or not at all. It's hard to watch Harold up in the truck, his sun-reddened face under the John Deere hat, in his blue Ag-Bag jacket, watching one machine, just overhauled for five thousand, going for two thousand. But the tractors are the ever popular green, and are much beloved by the buyers. Uncle Wally, down from Powhatan, buys the 4050. It's one he planned to purchase a few years back but couldn't make up his mind to get. Harold bought it instead, since he makes up his mind fast. Wally jumped into the bidding at the end, when it was already up around 18 thousand, and took it up to 25, an excellent price, but certainly what the well-kept tractor was worth. What motivated him? Family loyalty? A second chance at the tractor? Finally accepting that green beats greenbacks? Down in the crowd with Jason and Elaine, I shake a dozen hands, folks that want to make themselves known—farmers from around the state, family friends.

It's too hot, too crowded. I go inside for a short nap but wake up hours later to the sound of the auction almost under my window. They've moved up by the house, to the calf hutches and the feed tanks, the crowd diminished to folks who want to bid on the final items.

One young couple from South Carolina lingers until the end to bid on items from the milking parlor. He's just starting up and bought lots of cows and equipment at this sale; she has a little boy at home, maybe another one on the way. Milk prices are going down in his state, too, but he's optimistic, plans to get into the raw milk market, bottle his own, and sell it in Atlanta. He thinks they'll do okay. We hope so. Elaine wishes them luck, and she means it. Jason and I watch them drive away. They're our age.

The cousins order pizza, and we eat a late supper, wondering how many cows will be left to be milked tonight. Through the window, we see the auction tent lit up. Inside, the tabs are paid and tallies are being made. The boy who bought the 7020 tractor exits the tent, turns to his friend. "Well, that's done. All we have to do now is tell Jeannie."

We eat church-lady pie—chocolate, coconut, sweet potato. Loretta and Lorraine go out to milk the cows that used to be ours, and Jason and I feed calves. Number 13-A, never bottle-fed, takes eagerly to the bottle, though she has to be braced in a corner so she can stand still. Norton holds the bottle while I hold the calf, a fine $500 calf, one day old. I help to get the last of the cows into the parlor, a short milking, only half the usual hundred, and finish before ten o'clock.

I marvel at the great soft-eyed beasts, at their docility, their willingness to cooperate over the ages with their human partners, the work they do for us, the work we put into them. "Don't get too sentimental about cows," warns Norton.

"Don't worry," I say. "I may sound like an idealist, but deep down, I'm a pragmatist. Cows are too much work."

We start for the house; the moon is bright enough to put the stars in shade, but we can make out the blur of the Milky Way. It reminds Norton of nights on visits to the country when he was a boy: "I used to lay there and think about how far you could travel out in that direction toward that star. The idea of a boundless universe was too much for me. I went inside."

"Something most of us avoid thinking of," I say, "Like mortality."

"It's worth a minute or two of your time," says Norton.

When we come in, cousin Twila announces that the sale reports are in. "Elaine's happy," she says. "That's all I need to know." Harold comes in from feeding and picks up the final tally sheet. "Hallelujah!" he says. It looks like they'll have something left over after they pay off the debt. For two people who have been on their feet all day, who've had no chance to talk to each other, to process the fact of selling off their lives—who have also just put their house under contract to a man who has soft hands, no farmer—Harold and Elaine look good. They're beaming at one another, happy to be on the other side.

Thursday

Time slows down. There's one milking in the morning before the last cows are loaded onto trailers. The rest of us sit by the woodstove, moving closer and further from it as the contrary spring temperature demands. Twila and Elaine enter the cow sale statistics into a spreadsheet so they can take averages, make sums, and reference specific cattle.

"If it came out bad," says Norton, "There would be just one way to look at it, but good has many facets."

Farm Service Agency, the lender that holds the mortgage on the farm, calls to get the sale results. Harold says they rarely deal with a sale like this one—too often, the farm, the house, the cows, the equipment all go, and there's not enough money left to go around to all the creditors. By wisdom, providence, or great good luck the Alderfers quit now, while they were ahead enough to have a small retirement. And yet, there's something noble about farmers who plow themselves completely under, still hoping that the weather, the market, some miraculous turn will bring them through. They are not practical, like roosters who crow when the flock is gone.

The decision to sell, and the discussions that attended it, happened weeks ago. I came upon Jason sitting with Elaine on the gator, the last hutch of calves still unfed and bawling, the big dog Bruno lying beside them, the battered orange tom sitting on Elaine's lap. I stood beside them and listened to their talk for awhile, petted the tomcat. *What might have been? Don't second guess yourself—did Daddy want me to come back? We'll need to find something new to get excited about. Daddy says there's nothing sadder than a farm when the animals have gone.*

Folks are loading up equipment all day, and a low-slung possum-belly cattle truck backs up to the corrals. Outside the kitchen window, the sixty by forty blue and white striped circus tent has collapsed into a tiny packet that would fit into the trunk of my Corolla. In the evening, I play Scrabble with the three sisters, something I'd imagined since that time, years ago, when Jason talked about his mom and aunts, what a riot they were, how they were best friends and liked to play Scrabble together. Elaine stays up until eleven; she can sleep in tomorrow.

Friday

When Elaine sleeps in, she doesn't open her eyes until seven. When I come downstairs around nine, she's still in pajamas and a robe, and smiling. We have a pot of soup for lunch, then sit around the table until two o'clock, and joke, "Well, who's going to scrape the cow-lot, get the cows up for milking?" I let our chickens out of the pen to rummage through the compost heap, but they get interested in the mulched flower beds and I have to lure them back to the pen with scraps.

Jason and Elaine leave with Harold in the afternoon. His friend is selling an antique John Deere Crawler, with caterpillar treads, and Harold has decided to buy it. After all, he's down to just three tractors right now. He takes it for a test drive and makes a down payment, and both men get teary-eyed and hug over the transaction. They drink lemonade and talk and talk.

When Jason finally gets home, we follow the hard-packed logging trail back into what used to be the woods, find comfort in the trees still left about the stream, and admire the logging machine's pincers, like a beetle's. We visit Jason's favorite old waterfall, its remaining holly tree. Today it's just a trickle. Maybe it will be the last time we come back here, so he says good-bye, just in case.

We're glad that Harold bought the Crawler, will have time now to enjoy tinkering with his remaining tractors, and that he's already looking forward to a job with a John Deere dealer. It's what's enabled him to leave, to think of life without the farm. Those other farmers, who try to stick it out, who lose everything—I think it's because they can't imagine another way of life, can't bear to do so. On the way back, Jason stops in the field to meditate over the seven-bottomed plow that nobody wanted to buy. Large farmers don't plow any more; small farmers want something smaller. He figures how it could be cut down to three blades, for plowing a garden, perhaps. As we walk back to the house, we remark how quiet, clean, and uncluttered the grounds are. Even the smell of fresh manure has begun to dry up. "It's like someone's grand estate," he says. "It's not a working farm any longer."

Jason wants to show me how to drive a tractor, and I finally agree. It doesn't seem dangerous anymore. Elaine once told me she'd never learned to drive one because she knew that would mean she would have to—and she had enough work to do already. Jason tried to teach me once before, in an enormous brute of a tractor, but the one we try this time is smaller, more manageable—I don't have to throw my arm out to switch gears, and it's almost fun.

Elaine has grilled steaks for supper and sits easily in her chair. "I feel better already," she says, remembering falling milk prices and dry years. "I used to sit at this table with so much tension." Later, we play croquet with Lorraine on the freshly mowed lawn of the estate. She turns out to be a crack shot and defeats us roundly.

Jason and I take the second half of our walk out into the dusk. We walk out past the space that Harold planned to make into pasture, and we check to see if the wheat's heading up. There's too much to do on a farm for one man. "I don't think he'll miss the cows," says Jason. Harold isn't precisely a herdsman: he comes from a line of craftsmen, his father a cabinet builder. He always loved machines and, as a child, asked Santa for a manure spreader. The tractors Harold just sold were noteworthy for the good condition in which he kept them. His new job will suit him well.

Jason, in his own way, continues the tradition as a technician as a computer programmer, but he's got a problem: he's half Erb, his mother's side, half pioneer. His outdoorsmen ancestors gave him a heart too big for a city lot. He wants open spaces: Nebraska, Minnesota.

We find ourselves in the front lawn, under the stars, where we sat the first weekend he brought me down to the farm, when I felt a new glaze on the surface of my soul, thin as butter spread on toast, a feeling that I knew could develop into home. I marvel that we had the chance—and second chances—to be together. In some ways, this place feels almost more like home to me than my own home—vicariously, perhaps. I've absorbed Jason's attachments to his place, to his extensive and quirky family. The little brown house on the hill in Indiana is always dear, will always be home, but I've never depended on it or related so deeply to it as Jason does the farm. His attachments go back even further, to the farm he remembers from early childhood, his purest sense of home, though his parents didn't own it. It's harder to follow him in this—I've driven up the driveway of that old farm once or twice but never walked the place. It's being divided, hidden under houses. I know from his stories that there's a hill, somewhere, perfect for flying kites and watching stars as you lie on your back, while the cats from all their kingdoms gather round you purring. And a pond that he dreams of often, sometimes dry, sometimes full, sometimes bursting the dam, or disgorging bookshelves. It's a primeval, primordial attachment.

I say I have nothing like that. I have been convinced that there is no real sense of a place that's home for me, that I carry it on my back like a turtle's shell, in my heart like a tiny pearl. But within the month it will come to me, rush at me from a great distance, like the sea returning in a tidal wave to the empty seafloor, scooping up the gasping fish. Memory can hit you like that, out of nowhere, leave you breathless and clinging to a palm tree. We will sign a contract on a house of our own, start planning how we want to fix it up, what we'll do there, how it will be. I'll say, "I want to stay somewhere for more than two years." And the wave will hit.

I think most of us have a place, one place where we've belonged forever, the first place of memory, no matter how dim. I was six when we left the little white house on Miller Road, but I remember the wallpaper: trees and bridges, countryside scenery in repeated prints of gold and dust. I remember a bush where violets hid, the great stone cap of the well, the Adirondack chairs beneath a tree that branched low so that little girls could climb it. The cement walk in the back, the porch-rail boxes of marigolds, the grey cat buried in the backyard. The feel of it was buried so long, forgotten, that the renewal of the memory will make me weep.

I'm glad that Harold and Elaine have a little time before they move to enjoy their home, all cleaned up and without so much work. They don't have to leave quickly, ashamed, broke. "Someday," I tell Jason, "We'll tell our children about the big old house with the peacock on the front door."

Saturday

The Alderfer family takes an outing on a Saturday afternoon—for the first time in memory, Harold doesn't have to scrape the cow-lot. We drive a few hours east to his home community, Denbigh, Virginia, to see a play by the local Mennonites in the old Yoder Barn, which has been gentrified into a performance space. This neighborhood is where my family comes from too, where my first small house still waits on Miller Road.

In the back seat, just kids for now, Jason and I listen to Harold's stories. He tells about an inept farmhand—a real person, he assures us—who artificially inseminated some heifers. "Which bull did you breed them to?" asked his boss. "Oh, that one called Test. That's what it said on the pipette."

"Same guy was driving along with his buddies when one pointed out the window. 'That's where my taxidermist lives.' 'No kidding,' says our guy. 'I take my taxes to H & R Block.'"

Until today, Harold hasn't been able to drive himself further than a few miles at a time. He's prone to falling asleep at the wheel. Just a few days past the departure of the cows, the narcolepsy is wearing off.

Down at the Yoder barn, Harold knows everyone, can't take a step without falling into conversation. He remembers which man had the GR painted out of his Keep Off Grass sign fifty years back and remembers that the culprits used tin snips the second time around to remove the replaced letters. He reminds a few pillars of the community of other exploits, and at least one complains, "You're not supposed to remember that stuff anymore, Harold!"

The actors portraying the early days of the Denbigh colony look so normal, so right in their coverings and plain clothes. With their hair tucked under coverings and modest cape dresses, the women match photos of my ancestors. The contours of their Swiss-German Mennonite faces, the way they carry themselves—their voices must sound the same, too. I get nostalgic for this simple, rural world, then remind myself that this was never *my* life, this green colony. By the time I was a child in Denbigh, it was paved over, and no one farmed any more.

Sunday

The chickens aren't eager to return to the car for the trip home. They haven't finished eating all the vetch in the peacock pen, and they've barely scratched a hole in the enormous compost heap nearby. Their dusty run in our backyard can't compare. We're able to provide them with better accommodations than cardboard boxes for the return trip, however. One of the sheds yields an old-fashioned chicken coop, the kind that city people buy in antique shops and top with glass for a coffee table. Its wooden bars provide ample ventilation. We corner the chickens and pop them one by one through the hatch on the top. When we snap it closed, they hunker down, resigned to the journey ahead. We belt ourselves into our seats and bump down the winding driveway, the farm slipping away on both sides of us.

8

House

Briery Branch, Virginia

On the day we see the *For Sale by Owner* sign, it's official: we are not house-hunting. We're resting, recovering from the Alderfer farm auction. We're returning to the scene of our first date, the Hone Quarry dam in the far corner of the county, where Jason took me to hear tree frogs, since there are none in town. Today, we're not cruising past all the houses in our price range or arranging walk-throughs to see the houses in our price-range with Pepto-Bismol pink bathrooms, soggy evidence of bad drains, scraps of land on rocky hillsides fit only for goats. We've even considered houses in town: Houses between houses. Houses with weak foundations. Houses with leaky basements. We are not looking for real estate today, but we can't help noticing the sign by the road and the little house back by the woods. We arrange to see it.

No one has lived here for five months, since Mrs. Miller died and left her estate. This house is far from perfect. The old metal roof leaks. The asphalt siding in faux brick pastels chips in places, tempting compulsive fingers, giving entrance to wasps. Ceilings in the bedrooms and living room have spots from water damage and, in one place, a hole. The place reeks of mothballs scattered through the crawlspace to repel the skunks and groundhogs who dug under the foundation, hunting for real estate of their own. "And," says the man who shows us the house, "Water used to run down the cellar stairs when it rains, but we tightened the door, so that shouldn't be a problem any more." That's good, we think. At least it has a dry cellar.

I ignore this litany of problems. We see the other features, attributes of our dream house. The place has an air of gathered anticipation. Doors wait to be opened. Months from now, we'll unearth a list we made when we started the search. This house fulfills every item on the list. The small rooms feel large in their emptiness, full of light. A chimney rises through the living room, so we will be able to have a wood stove. The open kitchen has plenty of counter space, remodeled for a woman who understood that the kitchen should be the biggest room in the house. The bedroom windows face the sunrise.

Outside: An old chicken house. An abandoned outhouse, a two-seater painted bright red, full of tomato stakes. A pint-sized storage barn. A workshop with a little woodstove inside and a potato cellar beneath. A pole barn. Irises everywhere, ready to bloom. Acres of woods, with rumors of morel mushrooms and ginseng. The man, one of Mrs. Miller's sons, tells us we can explore the woods while he mows the narrow road frontage, if we want.

We follow one of the paths toward the sounds of water until there it is—Briery Branch, winding down from the mountains, half-awake, flowing over half of its rocky bed, the rest of the river rocks smooth and bare at our feet.

"We have to go back," I tell Jason, unable to stand by the stream for more than a moment. "Quickly! I'll be too disappointed if we can't have this place."

The house becomes ours by grace, magic, miracle, or our willingness to pay the asking price here at the height of the 2006 housing bubble. There's some careful numbers crunching, a rush to get the surveyors to finish their job, quick, while a good interest rate is still available, a little help from our folks. As we sign the papers, the lawyer takes every opportunity to joke about how we'll be paying "for the next thirty years." It's okay, I tell myself. The house has been here for at least eighty-five.

This place has plenty of history but few ghosts. The Javins brothers, a pair of soldiers, fell in love with two women from Briery Branch and returned after the American Civil War to settle on this land. Among other businesses, they had a sawmill and a distillery, where they made legal whiskey for the government. Their descendant and the last resident of this house, Mrs. Miller, lived here most of her life. This house was built around 1922 when she was a child; she raised her family here. She left her curtains, her flowers, and a kitchen with good counter space for us.

I feel the memories of someone else's presence the first summer, while I spend most of my days here alone, before the house is fully ours: little creaks and shiftings, doors swinging open. But soon Jason planes the doors and we learn the tricks of latching them.

Our neighbor, one of Mrs. Miller's daughters, asks if the living room floor still shakes. It does—we have to brace it up to support the weight of our new wood stove. Sometimes, she tells us, her grandfather would get fired up with drink, and he'd dance. Then the floor would really tremble.

Instead of ghosts, our little acreage holds physical reminders of the past. The fringes of the woods are full of rusty implements—an ancient harrow and planter—and abandoned household goods: bedsprings, an enameled cookstove. The chimney of the original house, built just after the Civil War, still stands down by the woods. It's made of river rock laid so expertly that, even though the mortar dissolved years ago, the stones still balance upon each other. It crumbles a bit more each year, as the roots of maple trees on either side of it heave the ground. The biggest one, a huge sugar maple, grows where the living room must have been.

Later, I will learn that my own people's Civil War history connects to this corner of the county, too. Just beyond Narrowback, the mountain that we see through our kitchen window, is Briery Branch Gap, a passage through the mountains into West Virginia, a back way out of the Valley. Over 2000 pacifist Mennonite and Brethren men and boys slipped through these hills during the war years to escape conscription into the Confederate military where they would be forced to bear arms in a battle they felt wasn't their own.[6]

Our family stories don't follow specific ones of these boys but remember the tales passed down by grandmothers and aunts who lived through those years: Elizabeth Swope Suter, whose baking dish sits in my cupboard, Aunt Mag, namesake of Aunt Maggie, who gave my grandma Janet a tiny pair of silver sewing scissors in her childhood, which I now use for embroidery. Susanna Virginia Suter, a child during the war, who traveled north with her family after the burning, Lydia Wenger, who stayed in the Valley during winter starvation that followed, and my great-great-aunt Katie E. Wenger, descendant of both Suters and Wengers, who wrote down those histories in her old age. All of them, simply stories now.

Before we move in, talking to a potential insurer, I get confused. I misremember the siding on the house. My memory tells me that it's white clapboard, so I have to call her back and correct myself. I won't understand why until a cousin visits and says, "It's just like your house on Miller Road, with those windows above the front porch." The universe snicks into focus. Our new house is a close match to that first house of my memory, down to the violets in the meadow out back. All it needs is white clapboard siding.

I'm having fits over finances this summer, determined to get new siding on before winter. White siding. Is my agitation to save enough money rooted only in aesthetics, a wish to cover up the awful faux brick, or is there more to it? Am I trying to make a time machine out of this house, to go back somehow to childhood? I don't remember being happy, but I must have been. I was home.

Water

Besides the old trash heaps in the woods, there's the stuff that washed in during the flood of '85. Families whose houses washed away combed these woods for their lost possessions, but the useless things were left. Sometimes we take a trash bag with us when we go for walks in our woods. We can always fill it with our findings—old bottles, someone's broken dish drainer, scrap metal.

Months later, in the fall, when the stream has woken to a river, we watch the tumult of water churning, pounding away at the bluff where I stand gasping. I don't have a scrap of buyer's remorse; I have buyer's awe. This river is ours, though it's much easier to say we own it when we can wade across without risking our necks.

In the dry days of summer, when we first came to this place, the river slept low in its bed. We could walk far back through the poplar wood to visit its visible branch, a backwoods meander shriveling to pools. But with heavy rains on the mountains, it refilled to its banks and expanded into a wide torrent under our neighborhood. It rose up through the gravel of our cellar floor in a muddy swirl.

Water doesn't run down our cellar stairs, as we were told. That leaky old door never kept the water out—it keeps the water in. We push it open and wade through the risen river in our old rubber farm boots, understanding now why the furnace and water heater are elevated to waist-level.

When Jason rolls the cover off of the well, we see our reflections less than five feet down. We live on top of a river, our house piled on the lattice of stones that keeps us from washing away, skirted by a layer of lawn and shrubs, a floating land. If the chickens scratched too deep, I say, they would fall in. Jason calls this fantasy; I call it emotional reality.

Our well is built the old-fashioned way, hand-dug and lined with river rocks. It's probably no different from the well where, during the Civil War, my own Many-Greats Aunt Mag Suter buried the family's money. Mag is remembered as wiley, formidable. She's the one who concealed the horses in a thicket on the ridge, who could diagnose diphtheria and treat typhoid and measles better than the doctor.

When a band of young soldiers seized the pies she was baking in their outdoor oven, she scolded them and made them sit down and wait while she served them pie, properly. She taunted another group of men who came searching for her father, Daniel, to conscript him for the army—following them as they searched the house, chiding them to be careful with their candles, taunting them as they hunted for him in the attic, suggesting that they search for Daniel in a big jug. They were looking for money as well as for Daniel, but they didn't think to dig around the well.

I put the rubber boots back on to wade across new streams in the forest, to Briery Branch. A weasel humps and hurries along the opposite side of the river, veering up and down the new, deeper cut of the bank before disappearing into the grass, perhaps searching for its washed-out home. Back at the house, we can see the fresh dirt at the foundation where the groundhog, flooded out of her burrow down by the pole barn, tried to open her old hole into our crawlspace. Jason had filled the hole with rocks, and the biggest boulder stymied her. We see where it tipped and smacked her on the head. Perhaps she moved in with her son, who lives on the higher ground under the old chicken house full of junk.

At the height of its rampage, Briery Branch changes course, straightening out a great bend of its path on the southeast corner of our land and ripping saplings out of the way. The fallen logs that once bridged it now tumble downstream toward the town of Bridgewater. We can hear the boulders grinding each other underwater, making sand that lines the shore when the water recedes. The bank crumbles. After the last big flood in '96, the Soil Conservation Service tried to contain the sometime river. They built a new bed and reinforced the banks with rocks and washed-out trees on the southeast corner of our land, but when the river is awake it chooses its own path.

When the water recedes, we explore the new bed the branch has cut on the southeast corner. Here, tree trunks thrust horizontally out of the rocky bank, spreading their root systems in the open air above the water. You can forget, for a moment, that these trees are here to buttress the Soil Conservation Service's structure. Believe, instead, that on this bank we are standing atop a mysterious land where the trees branch in soil and root in air, that under our feet grows a sideways poplar forest, that the autumn leaves of these trees fall according to their own laws of gravity—southeast, not down. Briery Branch, now calm, is full of drifting yellow leaves.

On a rational level, I don't fear the big floods. Our house is in relative safety, a few feet above the floodplain. We've bought flood insurance, just in case, but the bank trusted the location enough to not require any. The Briery Branch flood control dam is sturdy, tested, and well-monitored. In the big flood of '85 when the community was evacuated, there was a river down our driveway and a lake out back, and the neighbor's pigs had to tread water for a night to survive in their shed, but our house stayed dry.

And yet, does the river know these rules? It's the true owner of this floodplain. Given a season of extreme rains and hurricanes, the ground under our feet could wash away. The dam could burst. The lattice of stones that holds up this house could shift and grind to sand. We own the land, we have a financial contingency plan, but we can't control the weather. This land reminds us that life cannot be planned. It can only be lived. The past can rise up through your floor and overwhelm you. The forest is not what it seems. Breathe carefully when you think of these things. Even in mountain waters, there be dragons.

Woods

In the first years here, I grow straggly tomatoes, stunted peppers, lots of weeds, and one successful spiral of herbs. I abandon most of Mrs. Miller's flower beds to the wire grass, concentrate on the one around the house, and try to keep it mulched and weeded. I settle the chickens in the old outhouse. I wonder how this old two-seater compares to the facilities that Lydia Brenneman Wenger used in her day in Linville Creek. The stories don't tell us, although they do remember that during the war, Aunt Mag hid the silverware in the Suter outhouse, and that hungry soldiers took Lydia's whole flock of chickens for their dinner.

After they left, she found a hen that the soldiers missed, caught it, and stewed it for the family to eat, but when it was ready, the hungry soldiers returned. They took it outside and gathered about the cookpot to devour the bird. They could have been Union or Confederates; the story doesn't say, and both armies fed their hungry soldiers with whatever they could take from the fertile Shenandoah Valley—cabbages, sweet potatoes, apple butter—more than we manage to scratch out of our backyard garden.

We buy a new roof, so we're no longer threatened by water from above. Together, we nail down sheets of corrugated metal to replace the workshop roof. Jason, in his element, replaces corroded pipes, rewires the kitchen stove, plumbs an ultraviolet filter for the drinking water, fixes the leaky sink, lines the chimneys, installs a woodstove, puts in a half bathroom upstairs. I cheer him on, hand him tools, and occasionally squeeze into spots he can't crawl into. I cook and, when not too exhausted from teaching, write a little. But we're still waiting for the promised morels.

I watch for them each April when the ground first warms after spring rains. I'm as daft for mushrooms as a hobbit, so the rumor of morels in the woods keeps me tramping through the undergrowth, searching the leafy duff. Growing up, I'd find an occasional morel in our Indiana woods. The sight of one wrinkled cap at the roots of a beech would start a hunt. We'd fry them in butter. The flavor is indescribable. It's a past you want to return to again, and again.

I study the signs for morels: watch for poplar leaves as big as squirrel's ears, go hunting just after the spring beauties bloom. I rely most on a modern sign: when Virginians start posting sightings on the Internet morel forum halfway through April, I start combing the woods. I find plenty of detritus from past floods—the seat of a chair, broken glassware, someone's rusted out water heater—but no morels.

Looking at the ground so much, I meet each wildflower as it starts to bloom. My mother knows all of them by sight, but I need a book to remember their names. First, the spring beauties, their long-petaled daisy cups rising out of a single scalloped leaf. Star chickweed, which looks like a signet ring, making me think that it ought to be Solomon's Seal. Solomon's Seal, a row of tiny bells on an arching branch. Wood anemone, which I mistake at first for the rumored ginseng. But no morels, even after heavy rains.

The soil in our woods is sandy, built up from eons of rocks grinding each other in floods. It dries out quickly, so it's hard to imagine morels leading wet, secret fungal lives down in it. There's water further down, where the sycamores can siphon it through their deep roots, making them massive over hundreds of years, rising up under their dappled skin high into their white naked branches. In late summer, if you stand quietly, you can hear the sycamores shedding their bark.

The Millers logged out the oaks from this forest, leaving mostly sycamore, poplar, maples, and white pine. A few hemlocks still struggle against the woolly adelgids, but most of them have fallen. An invasive tree, ailanthus, crowds the opened spaces with spreading root systems and flimsy, fast-growing trunks. We can't save the hemlocks from the woolly adelgids, but we can fight back the ailanthus. We cut swathes of these foul-smelling trees down, poison their stumps, wash the stink off our hands. There are always more to cut.

In April, I have no trouble crisscrossing the woods to seek morels, but within a month the greenbrier and invasive multiflora rose will stretch out their thorny tentacles, making the woods impassable. The place is called Briery Branch for a reason. We have ranks of black raspberry along the edge of the woods, a few of the ground-running blackberries they call dewberries, and a patch of wineberries (yet another invasive species) that promises to take over the woods if we let it.

It isn't just non-natives that threaten our trees: last year, Briery Branch carved out the bank from under an enormous maple, and it toppled down into the stream. Windstorms took down an ancient pine far back in the woods and the old apple tree in the meadow. We harvest the ones that make good firewood.

Jason finally discovers morels around the roots of the apple tree with Pierre's help. Pierre, our grey cat, a mix of practical tabby and aristocratic Russian Blue, came to us in our second year here. He's a transplant, too—a non-native species. A former housecat, he arrived on a day when the neighbors were sighting their rifles, shooting intermittently all afternoon, and Jason was driving the roaring tractor to haul mulch. The cat, terrified, crouched all day in the jungle of mint by the back porch.

For the first few weeks, he could only run across the yard in short sprints the length of the hallway in his city house, but within a season he chased squirrels across the meadow. He runs to greet us when we get back from work, the little purring heart of our home. Pierre plays Whack-A-Mole, watching the soil pushing up where a mole tunnels, his whole body quivering, until finally he pounces, plunging his paws into the dirt. I saw him catch a mole once. He tossed it around the lawn. Its tiny star hands grasping madly at the air, its long snout bare, it squealed until Pierre let it fall too near its hole and it escaped into its underground home.

Pierre is hunting moles where the apple tree once stood. Jason stops to pet him and sees a wrinkly headed mushroom in the grass, the kind I've been stalking for weeks. He runs inside to pull me away from the papers I'm grading. He tells me to drop everything and come out. We find almost two dozen yellow morels in lines along the old apple roots, enough for a meal.

What makes these little lumps of quick-decaying flesh so significant? We treasure them so. Perhaps it's because—like wineberries and the sound of shedding sycamore—we cannot buy them. We can only hope, then receive them as a gift. They are true wealth. I fry the morels in butter and serve them with nettle pasta. In seventeen more years on the property, I won't find another morel on the property.

We savor these gifts of the land but don't know real hunger, like the people of the Valley experienced after The Burning in September 1864, when Sheridan laid waste to the breadbasket of the Confederacy, burning barns and mills filled with the year's harvests—most of them brought in by the women and old men. Grandmother Lydia and Isaac Wenger's mill was burnt, and Isaac begged to be allowed to take a few barrels of flour to feed his own family through the winter. The soldiers allowed him to enter the mill only after it began to burn, so he tore open a corner of the building, rolling out seven barrels before the soldiers told him that was too much, allowed him to keep two, and rolled the rest back in to be burnt. Three of their barns were burnt, and the fourth, Aunt Katie writes, was saved by the hired woman, who pretended to be insane to frighten the soldiers away.

As winter closed in, Isaac shared their meager supplies with the neighbors. It wasn't enough to last, Lydia cautioned him. "Then we'll all be hungry together," he responded. Somehow, most of them made it through the winter, though Isaac's father,

Joseph, who had been in poor health, never recovered from the illness made worse as he strove to save his own barn from burning.

The Suters didn't try to stay through the famine. Instead, they joined Sheridan's wagon train to seek a place to stay in Lancaster, Pennsylvania, sleeping in the open on their way, trying to guard their horses. Daniel's was stolen even though he slept holding the bridle; someone cut the harness. Emmanuel Suter found odd jobs to support them, and Aunt Mag helped him to butcher a hog. Little Susanna Virginia and her brother went to school that winter, but she was terrified that the family would return to Virginia without her, and she had to be reassured each morning that they would not forget her when it was time to go home to their empty farm in the Valley.

Nettles

Nettles grow on abandoned homesteads and thrive on our land near the old chimney. They, like our cat, are non-native. They traversed the Atlantic with someone who knew that nettles will keep you alive as your winter supplies begin to run out. They rise up early in the spring, chock full of calcium and vegetable protein. They'll cure what ails you: allergies, blood pressure, rheumatism, and baldness. They also sting. If I forget to wear long pants when I walk by the old chimney, I'll come back smarting from the histamines on the tiny hairs that fur each leaf.

I once made an evil-smelling hair tonic from nettles poached from my high school's nature preserve. But now I find that they make good soup, chopped with potatoes or pureed with chicken stock. They make an excellent sauce for pasta. They're super-nutritious, like spinach on steroids. You have to pick them with gloves and boil the sharpness off of their tiny needles. Don't be sparing as you pick the patch: nettles grow like the weeds they are.

Supposedly, you can pick them bare-handed if you grasp them assertively. You can eat them raw: again, with an assertive bite.

Nettles, I reflect, are like debt. They grow exponentially and they sting. But they can help you get what's good for you. This house is good for us, even though we both have to work to pay for the mortgage and the repairs. We have to stay away most days to stay here. We have to build up worldly wealth to enjoy the real wealth of this place: its violets and morels, impromptu mockingbird concerts, chickens on the grass.

I push myself into challenging places, grasp the nettle, and take my introverted self into the classroom to keep things up here. Sometimes we have to weigh our different wealths: what if Jason left the nonprofit job he believes in so that we could pay off the house and be free while we're still young enough to travel, to farm? If we were free of this debt, what would I do differently with the wealth of time and home? I'd still teach—a little. Maybe I'd give my time to service, like a "good" Mennonite. Maybe, like my mother, I'd stay home and raise gardens, babies, live on God's time like a mystic, stop looking at clocks. Maybe I'd travel. Maybe I'd write, really write, a book a year.

Money has twice been the sole reason I stayed at jobs with bosses who made me scream primal screams as I drove home at the end of the day. It's why I sit and write a few lines, then lose my train of thought, thinking about work, even though the next class is an entire summer away. Thinking about money makes me shrink like the pools in Briery Branch did, one dry summer when the water table was so low that the stream disappeared underground. The trout fingerlings swam frantically in the final puddles, seeking a way out. Each time I visited the pool, the fish were smaller. So was the pool. One day, a heron flew away as I broke through the woods. It must have been a regular visitor, snacking on the largest fish first. Its beak was long enough to pierce your heart.

I've tried to break the need for money. I've given up scholarships, I've lived in cramped apartments on a part-time job, I've always had enough, but money's caught me now. We want this place. I think this place wants us. We live here, but it isn't ours yet. For twenty or thirty years, will we live a sort of half-life here while we chip away at the mortgage?

Nettlecroft, we jokingly call this house, one of many names. It is our home, our castle, our sting. Jason has a little land of his own. I've rediscovered a place I forgot I had lost. I worry about the cost, but I won't give it up. It matches all my principles, though they are principles that I still need time to grow into: Learn to weed and water the garden consistently. Keep my chickens happy. Get enough exercise. Try to use less fossil fuel. Write every day.

Living on our own little homestead is part of Being a Good Person, something that resonates with my Mennonite DNA, this residual sense of being an outsider, a need to live with a mission. If you can't be burnt in defense of true baptism, eat local. If you can't be an exile for your faith, try to suffer for your art. If you aren't tormented by disagreements with the state church, struggle against your dependence on the oil industry.

It isn't really fair to compare myself to pioneering ancestresses, driven from home, trying to make it in a new land. I won't die in a bloody frontier massacre like Anna Hostetler. I won't have fourteen children, like Susanna Virginia did in the years after the Civil War. I have more debt and less land. I garden, raise chickens, hang out laundry to dry, like these women did, but with one important difference. These things I want to do are the things they had to do. As Jason says, I'm like a domesticated cat that hunts because it wants to, not because it must. Pierre throttles everything that moves, devours baby rabbits, exhausts the moles—then comes into the basement and picks daintily at his specially blended chicken and rice cat food. We live in a time of choice and abundance, where our decisions so far have more to do with too many good options: shall we burn gas into town to go to the fundraising gala for the new food cooperative or stay home and make yogurt? I feel like I have to make up my own measures of morality for this time and place, and sometimes they seem trivial.

Home

When the Suters finally returned to this valley after the war, they found that their barn, though empty, was still intact. Emmanuel wrote in a letter to his father that some neighbors had "commenced to carrying off the property" and displayed hostility in other ways to the Suters, who had sworn an oath of loyalty to the Union to cross into Pennsylvania. Yet he wrote with optimism, hoping that the Confederacy would be forgotten. The year half a dozen homes here in Briery Branch fly Confederate flags, I wonder what he would think of the guy who drives through the neighborhood playing "Dixie" on his novelty car horn.

And yet, it's usually quiet out here, so far from traffic lights. I am just one of many denizens of these eleven acres, peculiar only in that I find reasons to leave them so often, roaming more frequently than the cat. When I am away, I feel a tiny tug on my breastbone, calling me home. When I am here, I dread leaving. On work days, I force myself into the car, though I know I'll enjoy the work when I get there. Is it pathological to wish to be at home? Is it unrealistic to wish for a way to make my living here? Sometimes I think I must be a work-shirker, or debilitatingly shy, or afraid of my real potential, when that deep desire to stay here, at home, settles over me.

The realities are so separate; the institutional lighting, climate control, papers, deadlines, numbers, grades, meetings, and conferences all disappear when I step from the car. Here is where the deep activities of life are shared. We make food, make love, sleep out our weariness, walk with Pierre in the woods. It is hard, some days, to convince myself that the other world exists. Right now, in the shade of the walnut tree, four chickens rummaging in the earth, the bees buzzing, Mrs. Miller's old-fashioned rose blooming in passionate red bursts, birds twittering in dozens of voices, the smell of sun-warmed grass, I cannot believe that the outside world has any substance. Here, life is growing greenly as it always has in places of peace, between wars.

What if I live here, like she did, for the rest of my life, stay on this land in this valley where generations of my grandmothers and great-aunts lived? Perhaps, in their time, more traces remained of the Haudenosaunee, Manahoac, and Monacan people who traversed this land near the time of European contact, and before them, the matriarchal cultures who hunted and fished and farmed on this land for ten millennia, moundbuilders whose names are lost in time, whose monuments my ancestors may have plowed into the fertile farmlands of the floodplain.

We are told not to concern ourselves with the things of this world. To my ancestors and to my conservative cousins in faith, "worldly" meant the things in town. Electronics. Immodesty. The things of that world are not the things of *this* world: the massive branches, filigree of leaves, blue sky beyond. I can't believe there's idolatry involved when I set my heart on this summer place. I am merely a creature at home. This is my heaven.

When I'm away, I sometimes wonder whether I'll find my way back, whether I'll somehow get lost in the land of artificial weather, of electrons and hierarchies, whether this time the portal will have closed, and the wardrobe will be just a wardrobe. Will I get back to our home beside the sleeping river, our home at the edge of the state, the edge of the forest, of the mountains, of the sky?

Sometimes, the clouds form another range of mountains in the west, distinct enough to climb. Once, driving home, I saw our own mountains turn as insubstantial as the clouds above them, lifting right off the fogged horizon, floating up, daring me to believe that they were real.

I make it back every time. When I slam the car door, there is the cat, rolling ecstatically in the dirt. The rooster crows. The evening breeze rolls down off the mountains. Supper won't make itself. The garden wants water. I'm home.

9

A Butcher of Conscience

I was poised to plunge my hand into a dead, but still warm, chicken. From the teardrop-shaped hole carved around its vent, I would pull out its viscera. I had never done this before. I took a deep breath.

It was a pivotal moment in my crusade for self-sufficiency, but in truth, I don't remember it. I can recall the trouble I had cutting an opening around the tiny puckered asshole of the first bird with my dull knife, and how my mother-in-law Elaine helped complete the cut and eviscerated the chicken for me. I dressed out the second one myself but can't remember the moment of choice when I stood poised to violate the dead. We had a day's work ahead and no time to hesitate.

Butchering day was supposed to be a spiritual transformation, where I would pay the true price for eating meat. There'd be guilt, red like the blood spurting from severed chicken necks onto the apple stump; awareness, dawning keen as the blue flames of the propane cooker where the scald water boiled. I would suffer with the chickens, and then I would Understand Where My Food Came From.

This plan was conceived after years of sitting at traffic lights behind poultry trucks, common in the Shenandoah Valley. They're jammed with fat chickens who gasp in summer, shiver in winter, and sow their feathers along the roadways in every season. Pairs of feet stick up, immobile, in many of the stacked crates, and I can only hope the dead are separated from the soon-to-be-dead at the processing plant. I used to buy the end product, boneless-skinless chicken breasts, in giant freezer bags at the grocery store, but that was before I kept hens as pets. How could I meet the eyes of sweet Emily or Phoebe while I still ate the flesh of their factory-raised relatives?

I started driving forty miles out of my way to a farm stand where I could pay double for pasture-raised poultry. Soon it made sense to take it a step further and pasture our own birds. We have a meadow out back, my husband Jason is a handyman, and his farmer parents were willing to teach us how to butcher. I ordered twenty-five broiler chicks.

After you dislodge the piece of flesh around the vent, you'll have to peel off coruscations of fatty tissue, amber colored gobbets, before you can follow the intestines up. Pull them out in a few handfuls without tearing them. Do not try to unravel them in a single strand; you will end up standing yards away from the chicken with your in-laws laughing. The intestines connect to the gizzard. It's lodged in the belly of the carcass close to the vent, not the throat. Sever the intestines and clean the gizzard. Cut through the tough red side of the organ just far enough that you can peel it back to remove the membrane-enclosed contents without puncturing the sac. Inside, there's green grass and yellow hop-clover, smelling sweet as a fresh-mowed lawn, along with sand and tiny stones.

Pull out any remaining guts and detach the liver from the web of tissues that cling to the chicken's back. Gently carve off the gall bladder. Do not puncture it. It is smaller than your finger but will spurt Christmas-green bile everywhere. Throw away a mysterious brown organ. Wash the liver. Collect the heart and wash it, too. Try to find the lungs. They're buried in the ribs in a non-intuitive place, but if you scratch around with your fingernails, parts of them will come off. They are red and soft. Pull out the windpipe and esophagus. You may have to loosen them at the neck stump, removing bands of fat and probing with your fingers until they break free. Don't worry about the craw. Elaine can't find it either. Throw everything but the giblets in the slop bucket. Wash the chicken, picking out any quills the men missed and squeezing off the pulpy pink worms of tissue that ooze from the pores where the wing feathers grew. Put the bird in the cooling vat. Repeat.

These six-pound carcasses, cooling titanics afloat in ice water, came to us as yellow chicks no bigger than the eggs they'd hatched from the day before. All twenty-five fit into a cardboard shipping container smaller than a shoe box. They sang.

"They're so cute," I cooed.

"No, they're delicious," said Jason, trying to protect me from myself. I chose names for the chicks—Rotisserie and Giblet, Buffalo Wings, and Barbeque—to remind me of their purpose, but they all looked alike. This would make them easier to kill.

Through a mix-up with the hatchery, we ended up with a breed of chicks we hadn't meant to get: Cornish-Rock crosses, just like the birds on the poultry trucks. Frankenchickens, bred to grow. Their genetic program told them they were starving, so the chicks mobbed the feed, quickly outgrowing the quart-jar chick feeders. They'd sit in the shavings under their heat lamp to eat, already too heavy to enjoy standing. Their chests and bottoms jutted out; they looked like watermelons. At two weeks, I took the biggest chicks, ones I feared would burst, to a shady spot outside in the grass and poked them to make them waddle around. I showed them worms and encouraged them to dig like my laying hens. A few learned to eat grass. Some snuck into the weeds to sit down, running away from exercise class.

By three weeks, yellow down gave way to patches of feathers on their tails and wings. As soon as the feathers spread to their heads, we put them out on grass permanently. They had grown too big for their cardboard pen and sullied their wood shavings as fast as I could change them. On hot days, the sweet stink in the workshop made them gasp like the chickens on the trucks. Jason built a grazing box and electrified it to keep the neighborhood dogs away. The chicks cheeped in dismay at the new grassy ground until I set the feeder into their box. Then they brightened up and continued to eat and inflate. We moved the box daily, leaving a swath of pecked and trampled grass behind, grass that would be blue with nutrients later in the summer when the rest of the meadow turned yellow.

We wrote the weights of the fattest roosters on the calendar: four pounds at four weeks. Nine pounds at seven. We emptied four hundred pounds of feed into their gullets. One died in a stampede during a hailstorm. Another grew slowly. He looked like the picture of a half-sized chick I found in an online 4-H presentation. "It will never catch up," read the presentation, "It is best to cull a chick this far behind." I named him Cully. He was lighter and faster than the others and would hop up on their backs to reach the feed long after they'd become somnolent bricks. I gave myself permission to pardon him at the last minute, but he caught up with the others by butchering day. Not even Cully could escape his inheritance. All of them lost their heads.

The fattest rooster went to the hatchet first. We took a picture of him, perfectly spherical, tipping nine pounds, ten ounces on my grandmother's baby scales. Even the smallest pullets were heavy enough to be independently viable, had they been born that day as human babies. While we waited for the water to boil, we set our victim on the grass. He shuffled around among the butchering implements, the board table, the cooling vat, the wheelbarrow, and then plopped down on the grass to await his fate. Later, I held his feet while Jason's dad, Harold, dispatched him with the ax. This rooster was a double-whacker. Don't make the mistake of swinging gently: try to split the apple stump.

When he stopped flapping, I handed him to Elaine to scald. I picked up his head. The tongue twitched and was still. I threw it in the slop bucket. Plucking his feathers, I was oddly hesitant to touch the neck stump, the site of the mortal wound. The process grew easier by the bird, and soon I was pulling feathers off in handfuls. After we'd collected a stack of bald carcasses, we left the killing and plucking to the men. Elaine apprenticed me as a dresser.

She showed me how to sever the feet at the first joint. The slop bucket soon filled with kindergarten colors, swarmed by iridescent flies: Yellow feet. Bright red combs. Pink, purple, and blue viscera. Green bile. Brown bits. White feathers. Elaine helped me snap off the thumb of the wing, a secret claw that you'd never notice under the feathers. With leathery skin and a rigorous program of diet and exercise, these birds could have been pterodactyls. But instead of wildness, they chose the easy genetic route, cast in their lot with humans, and opted for numbered, corn-fed days. Not that these particular chickens had any choice in the matter. By now, they were far too fat to fly the coop.

Elaine also taught me to cut off the oil gland above the tail, a tiny yellow sac that her Pennsylvania Dutch mother called the *schmutz tsepli*. None of us knew what it meant, though Jason's German dictionary confirmed that *schmutz* meant dirt or filth. I thought my dad's mom, born Beachy Amish and butchering through her teens, would know all about it, but she couldn't remember processing chickens. "*Schmutz* is grease," was all she knew.

I tried my grandmother on the other side, but she didn't think she had ever dressed a chicken either: "My mother didn't do that at home." But Grandma must have butchered at least once, because my own mother recalls fleeing from a headless rooster as a child. At home, Mom complained about touching frozen chicken breasts to make her lemon chicken recipe. She hated touching raw meat. I didn't cook meat until I left home, and it took me an entire afternoon with an old-fashioned cookbook to figure out how to dismember my first whole chicken. If I want to claim butchering as my heritage, I have to look back more generations that I know, or borrow Jason's inheritance.

By supper time, we'd entombed half the birds in the freezer and tucked the others, whole, in cooling tanks. I baked some fresh pieces of chicken. After a day of butchering, everything looked like meat. Jason's thumb, where he rested his chin, resembled a quarter of chicken waiting to be eased out of its socket and divided into thigh and leg. We were too tired and hungry to hesitate over the chicken dinner. Later in the evening, with the final pieces slammed into the perspiring freezer, we tallied it up: 137 pounds of meat, mostly bone-in. Twelve hours of work by four people. This was the strangeness of the day: to take a living, squawking bird of smooth white feather and bright eye, and transform it into a food commodity—thigh, leg, breast, tenders, just like you find in the store. Twenty-three little deaths. How far we came in one day, from the grazing pen to the freezer.

On a sunny January afternoon, half a year past butchering day, I rest not far from the apple stump with a smoky cat licking his claws beside me, the remains of my chicken cacciatore lunch cooling in the refrigerator. My laying hens forage around the backyard: Phoebe the speckled Sussex dustbathes in a patch of sun, the randy new Buckeye rooster struts for yellow Emily, and the rest chuckle as they rummage through the compost pile.

I feel no regrets for the killing of twenty-three young Cornish Rocks. I thought the job would be distressing, distasteful, transformative. But when my sister phoned after butchering to call me Lady Macbeth, I laughed. I felt no pangs of conscience, no blood on my hands, for butchering these birds. The largest died of fatness two days before the butchering, too heavy to hold up his head. I separated him from food and gave him cold water and a cool spot to rest, but it was too late. His respiratory system was only fit to support a bird half his size. We dug a grave. The rest were reaching the same level of grossness; they couldn't help their addiction to corn pellets, either.

If I have any qualms at all, it's for raising chicks with desperate hungers hard-wired inside of them, chicks that could never know how to be chickens. Next time, I'll butcher roosters with a history, even if they have a lower feed-conversion ratio and take longer to grow, even if they have enough personality to distinguish themselves. I'll raise chicks from a traditional breed like Javas or Rhode Island Reds. I'll pay for their feed and boil chicken broth in winter. They'll accept the harsh contract of domesticity, its protections and its price. The hens and one lucky rooster will live on, providing us with eggs and companionship.

Some of the more adventurous ones, lighter of body, stronger of wing, may escape into the woods. Perhaps, years from now, I'll stumble upon the feral chickens of Briery Branch in some sunny glade, teaching their young to fly and hunt, to leatherize their skins and unsheathe their secret claws. I'll reach for my net and spear, tightening my grasp on the power that makes us carnivores, the secret of making life from life.

10

The Last Worker

On the twelfth day of the first year of the Obama administration, as the nation's economy continued to crumble, we opened our beehive and found the colony dead.

Through most of the winter, we left the bees alone so as not to release the heat they generated huddled between their walls of honey. But when the temperature rose into the 50s, the bees could bear the air enough to take brief cleansing flights, and we dared to open the hive for a few minutes. We had plenty of unseasonable warmth this year—sunny days when the bees flew to gather maple sap, risen during the freezing night, draining through holes the sapsucker drilled through the bark. No bees were flying the afternoon we opened the hive, but we assumed they'd finished their business in the warmest part of the day. A few dead bees lay scattered below the hive, evidence of the cleaning efforts of the undertakers.

Even though the hive still had honey-weight when we hefted it, Jason decided to bring the bees a sugar syrup bailout. If the nectar flow is slow in early spring, even strong colonies can die of starvation. Jason pried up the lid and eased it back just enough to expose the winter feeder, a deep tray tucked into the box instead of a tenth frame of honeycomb. I anticipated the small eruption of bees that comes with hive-breaking and winced, despite my veil and gauntlets. No one emerged. We guessed it was too chilly for the bees after all, so I ladled the syrup quickly, sloppily, so that we could put the lid back on. My cup made a poor ladle, and syrup sludged between the frames and down the exterior of the hive. No matter, I thought. The bees would soon clean it up.

But then we opened the hive for a quick peek. Across the top of the frames, we found a scattering of dead bees. They'd been using a crack under the cover as a second entrance; perhaps they'd brought up their dead to dump on their next flights. But nobody flew up between the frames to see about the influx of light and cold. Jason prodded a bee cluster clinging near the top of a pair of frames, but instead of stirring into angry action, the bees dropped lifeless into the hive body. We beat on the sides of the box. No response. We pried off the top box, looking for survivors in the bottom half of the hive, only to find thicker clusters of unmoving bees and at the bottom, heaps of the dead. We'd lost the colony.

In winter, the bees cluster tightly to form a corporately warm-blooded sphere around their queen. The skin of the sphere is two tightly packed bees thick; the bees trade places before cold overcomes their ability to move. Inside the sphere, attendants gather around the queen, burning honey for heat by shivering. Maintaining a summery warmth of 64 to 90 degrees at its center, the cluster creeps from frame to frame as the bees empty the cells of honey. Sometimes, it's too cold for the cluster to move, or confused, it breaks into less efficient factions. Sometimes a virus will take out the bees—just a touch of dysentery could throw off the balance. Sometimes, the cold is enough.

On Inauguration weekend, the temperature dove below zero, 30 degrees lower than our average for mid-January, close to the record low. We thought the colony made it through the cold patch. A week later, with the volatile mercury reading 63 degrees, I went down to check the hive and found a handful of bees flying. Only one worker was on mortuary duty. She dragged a dead bee to the edge of the porch and then off, plummeting with the body. It wasn't enough to accompany the corpse to the ground; as soon as she righted herself, she tugged it through tangles of dry grass to a resting place several dozen bee-lengths away. I couldn't detect any difference in the new place or the body's position, but the undertaker seemed satisfied and launched herself up to the entrance to collect another body.

Must not be many dead bees, I thought, if they only need one worker to carry them out. But of course the opposite was true. So many bees had died that few remained to clean out the masses of bodies.

That would be my job. The day after we found the silent hive, I pried the boxes apart. I carried the pieces, still sticky from sugar syrup, outside of the bear fence to brush the bodies from the frames. The corpses fell around me in furry heaps, perfectly intact, as though their transparent wings would stir to life at any moment. I didn't bother with a veil or gloves.

Halfway through the top hive I found bees I couldn't remove. They'd burrowed deep into the comb seeking the final drops of honey at the bottom of the cells. Unwilling or too cold to emerge and move to a new frame of honey, they starved. I found a few scouts clinging to full frames of honey, frozen mid-search. They brushed off easily, but the starving bees had tucked themselves so tightly into the comb that I couldn't get purchase on their pointed abdomens, even with finger and thumb.

The last time I saw bees tucked so firmly into a comb, Jason held a nursery frame for me to check for new brood while a cloud of bees swirled angrily around our veils. At the edge of the frame, a new bee pushed itself through the remains of the wax cap on its brood cell, antennae twitching, legs wriggling in an ecstasy of sensation and motion.

When it finished hatching, it would turn and clean out its cell, then join its broodmates to tend the next generation. From the nursery, it would probably graduate to the honey-guzzling, wax-making chain gang. When it outgrew the ability to secrete wax, it would move on to housekeeping duties—distilling honey, breeze-making, and patrolling for intruders. If, however, it was to be an undertaker bee, it would bypass all these jobs and specialize in the proper disposal of the dead, removing trash if corpses weren't available. The final role for all workers is the same. They fly miles at a time, scouting and foraging for the colony until they grow too weak to return to the hive.

Winter bees live the longest, if they survive the cold; there's no foraging. Their sole job is to warm the queen. She's the reason for their existence, the cohering force in the hive, yet she's helpless without the workers. In early spring, they induce her to lay, carry her from cell to cell, feed her and clean her. She's self-sufficient only once: during her mating flight. I can't find the queen of this dead hive; she's probably in the tumbled mass of bodies collected on the bottom board.

I wonder if the bees realized when the end came. When we opened the hive on the first of February, one bee still stirred among the dead scattered atop the frames—an antenna, then a leg, in drunken motion. She was too weak to fly. Still, she tugged at the corpses around her, hoping—it seemed—to drag one last sister from the hive, to bury herself with it in the proper spot under the dry grass. Was death, to her, like any other bee's death, weary but working until the last, like the bees who try to hike back to the hive when their wings give out half a mile from home? Was her focus biologically narrowed to the job at hand?

Or did this little undertaker know, in some tiny part of her bee brain, that she was the only one left, that her civilization had collapsed beyond return? Did she panic as the scent of her queen faded? For us, it was no surprise: even experienced beekeepers lose a few colonies in winter. For her, it would have been the end of the world.

All through the fall, while the bees harvested the last of the heath asters, hoarding for winter, I put my faith in the political process. I knocked on doors, called strangers, cheered for a face behind the tinted windows of a motorcade, stocking up on change and yes-we-can. I thought a younger, compassionate leader might be enough. Now I fear for him, for all of us, and there's nothing left to do but wait massed together, sharing warmth, to see how cold this economic winter gets.

11

Field Notes Towards a Doctrine of Chicken

Theory and Methodology

These days, instead of praying, I watch chickens. This is not standard Christian practice, even for Mennonites like me, who have traditionally lived close to the earth. It doesn't even mesh with more eastern religious practices. A flock of chickens is no Zen garden, no smooth open space for meditation. A flock of chickens is a series of distractions, the ever-shifting motivations and pursuits of six greedy individuals with fifteen-second attention spans spending the afternoon together. It's day-care without diapers or time-outs. If my broken-beaked Emily came upon a Zen sand garden, she'd dustbathe—sand and feathers flying across the raked paths! In Christian bookstores, the suncatchers etched with inspirational messages do not have images of chickens. That dubious honor goes to falling sparrows, doves, soaring eagles and, unbiblically, hummingbirds.

I confess no great fondness for Christian bookstores, suncatchers, or inspirational messages. My spiritual life has not been enriched by inscribed bookmarks or personalized crosses. I'm barely comfortable with the prayers for all occasions collected in the back of the *Mennonite Hymnal*.[7] I'm skittish of prayers read aloud in church. Who is praying? The writer? The reader? The congregation? Who is putting words in whose mouth?

I try to justify my discomfort thus: As a member of an Anabaptist group, I shy away from both High Church forms and charismatic emotionalism. I'm fine with the Lord's prayer but prefer Luke's simpler version, without all the "thine is the kingdom and the power" business. I also like a simple prayer my father prays: "Let us be the hands and feet of Jesus." That's plenty form for me and enough words to cover everything that needs to be covered.

I try not to offer up words at all, when I can help it. I know too much about rhetoric. I prefer to offer up a walk back to Briery Branch, an evening by the fire, rhubarb wine with friends, a challenging yoga class, or an afternoon's chicken watching. This brings us back to the original point: the spiritual benefits of chicken watching, of which there are many. With my mind overtuned for metaphor, I watch the flock and glean clues for a theology that's all-natural, all-chicken.

Petition

As soon as they hear the house door open, or simply see me through a window, the hens begin to holler. They run out of their shack and line up at the fence, caroling. Even when it's clear that I am coming, a jug of water in one hand, feed and scratch grains in the other, they continue to call. Phoebe, the Speckled Sussex with a polka-dot petticoat, can't contain herself and jumps up and down, her beak turned toward Heaven—the direction from which the scratch grains fly when I throw them over the fence.

If the chickens are ranging in our backyard when I step outside, they rush across the lawn, their drumsticks pumping, wings flapping for balance. *Youyouyou!* they cry, *youyouyou!* I could almost mistake this for worship, but it isn't. Not true worship, anyhow. If I have nothing for them, they quickly lose interest. Their joy in me is connected entirely to what I can offer their stomachs.

One winter night, I didn't count the hens when I closed up the pen, and yellow Charlotte spent the night in our cold backyard, away from the heat lamp and the feathers of her sisters. When the sun rose enough for her to see—chickens are blind in the dark—she stood under our bedroom window and shouted until I crawled out from under the down comforter, thrust my feet into some boots, and lifted her back into the pen. She came straight to the source and didn't hesitate to ask.

Also: she knows where we sleep.

Original Sin

Chickens are not born evil; they are born raptors. They have claws and beaks and hunger and hierarchy. Factory chickens are bred to be docile and obese, but they'd still peck each other to death in the close quarters if they were allowed to keep their beaks. My hens, a little closer to the original jungle fowl, dinosaur fire still in the eyes of the Americaunas, only peck as a reminder. No one pulls out anyone's feathers. Rarely does anyone gets pecked until she bleeds. They have ample access to food and water, plenty of roost space, and about twenty square feet apiece in the chicken run. That's about three times the number of square feet alloted in theaters for each human audience member. The hens have a hierarchy, but everyone gets fed, and they snuggle together on chilly nights.

But they lack finer feelings. When our golden Americauna Belinda caught a cold, we separated her from the flock for a few weeks. She improved, staying down in our warm cellar, but then it flooded during the winter melt. I found her in the morning perched above the water, wet-feathered and mad as hell. I put her in a grazing box in the sun to dry, but while we were at work a dog attacked the box and got a mouthful of feathers. She was crouched in the undamaged corner of the box, trembling, when I found her.

I returned her to the secure run with the rest of the flock. She ran about squawking: *Everyone! Everyone! You'll never believe what happened! I've had the most horrible day!* How did they respond? They beat her up. That's compassion for you.

Communion

If you throw a wafer—well, a stale Ritz cracker—into the pen, Miranda will nab it. She's an Americauna, all beak and mane, no comb, and fearless. She'll sprint, cracker in beak, to the farthest corner of the run, pursued by a bevy of hens.

Methusaleh, the Rhode Island Red rooster, will stroll behind sedately. He outweighs any two of them together, but is too gentlemanly or too arthritic to interfere with the match. Miranda can't swallow the cracker whole and so she must drop it. Mama, the weighty White Rock, will shove in, snatch the cracker, and run to a different corner. It will break in half and Phoebe will peck at it until Miranda bops her on the comb. In this way, the wafer is shared, Emily, Methusaleh, and little Belinda catching the falling crumbs.

So much for the wafer. I haven't dared try them on wine. They'll swallow grapes whole, stretching their crops to avoid sharing.

The flock would have no problem with the doctrine of transubstantiation, the idea that the bread mystically becomes the Savior's flesh. Whenever they're set free, or escape, they run first to our compost pile and the first thing they'll seize, if available, are the leftover bones and deep-fried skins of take-out chicken. *If you are what you eat,* they might say, *Why not eat what you are?*

1. Given the opportunity, they will eat anyone—not just their Savior, and not just metaphorically.
2. Participation in communion is competitive.
3. June bugs trump wafers, every time.

Salvation

Chickens don't bother with guilt. I can catch them in flagrante delicto, tearing up a flowerbed, and they'll ignore my shouts. I can shoo them out, but they'll come back as many times as I chase them. If I don't want hens in the flowerbed, why did I let them out of their pen? Why, indeed? If God didn't want us to eat the apple, why was it in the Garden? I enjoy watching my chickens run free; what pleasure did God derive from watching Adam ignore fruit?

Chickens don't do guilt, so they can experience salvation only in its most physical sense. Like the day at our old place when I opened the screen door to see Charlotte and a red-tailed hawk rapidly parting ways, the hen squawking and streaking to wedge herself into the two-inch crack between the house and an old dog-house, the hawk flapping to a low branch of the maple. I chased away the hawk and went to soothe Charlotte. I had to pry her out of her hiding space—bold Charlotte with an orange eye, a yellow eye, and a rooster spur on one leg, Charlotte who raised her hackles and attacked the fence when a visiting dachshund got too close—Charlotte trembled and crept into the doghouse and refused to come out.

I left her and went to rally the troops. Phoebe and Emily, crouching in the bushes, soon emerged to kick gravel around in the carport. But Miranda was gone. We searched the shrubs around the house, the hedgerows, walked up and down the road and beat the shrubs again. The hawk must have got her, we agreed, then came back for another one. Maybe there were two hawks.

We searched all afternoon, and then went inside to make our suppers. Hours after the rumpus, just before dark, we heard a loud cry and rushed outside to see if the hawk had returned. It was Miranda, strutting up the sidewalk hollering, *I'm back! Where are you guys?* There was great rejoicing and we all rushed to meet her, human and fowl, except for Charlotte, who had to be carried up from the doghouse at bedtime and who hid inside the chicken house for the next three days when the others went out for their afternoon stroll.

Ritual Cleansing

My chickens spend hours in their purification rites. They scratch deep dust-holes and then nestle down into them, kicking dirt up over their backs, shaking the dirt through their feathers. If you come upon one suddenly, it's startling: a half-chicken, a chicken embedded in the soil, its eyes half-closed while the dirt seeps down between its feathers. They prefer the loose dirt of flowerbeds above all other dirt, but they'll take any sunny corner of their chicken run if necessary. Lice can't get a foothold in the powdery dirt; I don't have to dose them.

The hens share their dustholes with each other, and a lot can fit in one dust-hole. However, if Methusaleh plops down in the middle of the bath, it's usually the more timid hens who end up building adjoining holes, even if they were there first. Then again, Belinda can and will defend her advantage, once she's dug in.

Pilgrimage

Last winter, at our rented house, the chickens weren't wholly comfortable in their low, roost-less, front-less hutch. Phoebe, believing in a better life, set out into the world and found the corner of the carport where we kept extra straw. She returned to this place faithfully each night to nest and had to be carried to her proper bed. "Think of the foxes," I told her, but she ignored me. Freedom was worth it. Soon Emily, and then Miranda and Charlotte—the whole flock at the time, followed her lead, and I'd have to carry two loads of chickens home each night unless I remembered to herd them to the hutch before dark. Phoebe resisted, ducking and running back to her corner. I had to shoo her with the leaf-rake. When we blocked the straw bale, two of the hens gave up and went home, but Phoebe and yellow Emily roosted amongst the flowerpots in the carport, keeping vigil.

This fall, at our new house, we refurbished the old two-seater outhouse into a deluxe chicken shack with proper roosts and nest boxes and egress to a large run. But we had two new hens and a rooster to shelter in this deluxe chicken shack; the original four remained in their hutch. Phoebe sensed the approach of winter. One afternoon, Jason left the workshop door ajar, and she led them inside. I found them there, gravely examining the circular saw and exclaiming to each other about the high ceiling and good lighting. I shooed them out, but promised that, as soon as they made peace with the new flock, they would be granted proper housing. Which brings me to

Ecumenism

The first time I integrated new hens into the flock, I was not particularly tactful. Phoebe and Miranda had traveled all day with us from Indiana in a cardboard box in the back seat of the car. We arrived home, travel-weary, after dark, tucked the two new hens into the hutch, and went to bed.

When the sun rose, all hell broke loose. Charlotte, used to queening it over her broken-beaked sister Emily, had no intention of giving up her status as top hen. Phoebe was larger and more clever, and Miranda had a bigger beak, but Charlotte was on her own turf. She turned out to be loudest, and used her volume to impressive effect as she chased them about the pen. She scolded and cursed for two days. The third day, she lost her voice and could only growl, but she had kept her crown. The new birds treated her with wary respect, as you might a psychotic extremist.

Seasons later, when it was time to move these four into the deluxe chicken shack with the new rooster and hens, I decided to give them plenty of room and time. I freed both flocks to roam in the backyard. Methuselah was eager to met the new hens and strutted back and forth between the separate flocks. The hens glared at each other across the grass. Over the next few days, in a series of short, quick competitions, they tested their strength against each other. They'd get up on tiptoe in each other's faces, beak to beak, their chests puffed out, trying to stare each other down. They'd exchange a swift peck or two, and within seconds one of the hens would bow to the other, who would hold her head up even higher before she strutted away.

Charlotte, however, refused to bow to the queen of the new flock, White Mama, an enormous broody Plymouth Rock. They sparred for five minutes before Mama tore a piece out of Charlotte's comb. Charlotte, instead of making proper obeisance, ran behind the storage barn and sulked for the rest of the afternoon. After that, peace reigned during the grazing sessions, though the rooster was the only one who talked to everyone.

It was time for the old flock to move in with the new. I invited Charlotte, Emily, Phoebe, and Miranda over to the new house and showed them the food and the water. They looked interested but left quickly; this was someone else's home. I closed their pen so that they couldn't return to the hutch at dark, left the Deluxe Chicken Shack open, and went out for the evening with Jason. After dark, I found all seven chickens roosting in the new house together. I don't know what they did or said, but somehow a plea was made, an invitation issued, or someone pushed and someone else gave in. Given enough time, space, and incentive, they came to an understanding.

Healing and Dying

At about the point in a person's illness when we Mennonites might hold an anointing service to dedicate them to God's care, chickens assassinate. I didn't understand this with my first three hens: Charlotte, her sister Emily, and the little white Leghorn, Anne. They seemed as innocent as the maiden Bronte sisters, eager to eat my offerings of grapes, tomatoes, and Japanese beetles, content to scratch all day in the dirt. Timid Anne was scarcely more than a pullet, a factory chicken with a docked beak that curled where it had been cut short so that she looked like she was whistling. She'd try to pluck grass tips and lamb's quarters with the phantom beak and fail again and again.

One evening, I brought my offerings to the pen to find a bright-eyed Emily and Charlotte unimpressed by the food and more interested in the dusty, wormish strands strewn about the run. I peeked in their hutch. Anne was clearly dead. I dealt with death in the most mature way that I could: I went and found Jason. I watched him gather up the pieces and shovel. Ann's vent prolapsed—not unusual for a young layer from a breed engineered to lay large eggs early. Her flockmates finished the business by unraveling her guts. We couldn't have done much for her. Standard procedure is to replace the defective bird.

For weeks afterwards, watching Emily and Charlotte on their journeys around the backyard, always together, peering around like a pair of nearsighted old women in baggy trousers, clutching their purses close and gossiping softly, I'd get cold chills. It was like discovering that the grandmother in the apartment across the hall has had a collection of stolen babies in her freezer all these years.

This will for murder may be a form of mercy. A year later, I saw the flock begin its funeral ritual for Charlotte, but I finished it my own way. They had ignored her developing idiosyncrasies: her tilted head, the way she walked in drunken circles until she couldn't even find her way back into the coop. But the night that Charlotte lost her balance completely and fell flapping as I helped her find the water, Phoebe flew forward with her beak outstretched and Methusaleh jumped down, kicking with his spurs. If I had not pulled the sick hen out of the way, they would have torn her to pieces. I have a little scar on my knuckle where Methusaleh's spur tore me. It was only time he ever kicked me.

The flock had a good point. By this time, Charlotte's head had twisted completely backwards and she couldn't eat or drink. She was too far gone for any of us to help. I asked Jason to help me. He dealt the death blow, because he can swing straight, but I held her still under the blade of his axe. She didn't struggle, and afterward her body didn't leap about as they say it should; she was already on her way out. I felt we did the right thing. I do not think that act of killing tarnished my soul. I am a pacifist; I also descend from generations of farmers. Farmers grow—and kill.

Joy

My chickens rarely wish to be anything that they are not. Sure, Methusaleh wants to be taller, but he stretches his neck and he is. Phoebe wants to fly and sometimes, under the proper conditions, she does. Either that, or she teleports—there's no other way she could get past the fence. No one even seems to care who is top chicken, after the matter has been decided. It is easy to keep them happy. Food, water, room to roam, grain and garbage for variety, crabgrass for salad, and good powdery dirt. They like to be let out into the yard so that they can rummage around in the bushes and chase grasshoppers, but they seem to be just as excited about running inside to the feeder, kicking pebbles around in their little run, or strutting outside to catch some sun. They lay eggs every day, but do not grow less proud; they cackle just as loud.

They teach me that I do not need so much, that it takes little to be deeply grateful, something as small as a fresh warm egg in my hand. When I watch them, peace settles. I like to imagine a God who looks upon me as I look upon my chickens: intrigued, absorbed, sometimes deeply disturbed, wondering what is going on in their tiny minds.

12

Eggs: A Short History of Infertility and Ducks

When you are a Granola Mennonite couple just getting started on a little homestead, free stuff is gold. So when my father-in-law called us a few days before the 2008 Virginia Mennonite Relief sale and asked, "You want some ducks?" we said, "Of course," arranged to pick them up at the sale, then hurried to research Muscovy ducks.

A few words first for the uninitiated about our relief sale: thousands of Mennonites in the Shenandoah Valley—from bonnet-wearing to Bible-thumping to Global Village to granola to college students—gather for a weekend of eating homemade donuts, potato chips, and Brunswick stew, watching church people grind cornmeal and churn ice cream, purchasing apples and grapes, and participating in conspicuous generosity at an enormous quilt auction, all to raise money for Mennonite Central Committee, a global relief organization.

After stuffing ourselves with pancakes for the good of the world, we went out to my father-in-law's truck to see the birds, who sat placidly in a wire cage, dipping their beaks into a coffee can of water. Stella was a blue-eyed white duck with a demure gray cape and a bandit mask of red skin. Black-and-white Stanley was larger and had a fright mask that covered his entire head in red knobs and warts. These caruncles are supposed to be very handsome—to ducks. A child visiting us sometime later had another opinion: "It looks like his *brain* is on his *head.*"

Muscovy ducks are perching birds with talons at the ends of their webbed feet. They fly, but won't fly away. They enjoy water, but just need a pan, not a pond. They don't quack—they just whisper and huff, and they are close enough to their wild roots to brood and hatch their own ducklings. Muscovies seemed right for us—low-maintenance, no-nonsense, quiet-in-the-land birds. A good match for a down-to-earth woman like me.

I never worried about my weight or my looks, beyond learning that long and straight was the easiest style for my hair. I liked natural fibers, knew how to wear makeup but rarely did, didn't have cramps, hardly ever had headaches, slept through the night, would eat anything (but didn't keep that processed crap around the house), and often found myself to be the more rational, less emotional half in my marriage with Jason. I balanced the checkbook and paid the bills, and my favorite color was brown.

I wore my good health like a virtue, without any conscious sense of entitlement. When we decided, in early 2009—the same time the ducks began nesting—that it was time to grace the world with our offspring, I was comfortably certain that the first would arrive soon, though I had no illusions about instant pregnancy. I stumbled into—and then quickly out of—the obsessive mommy-wannabe Internet forums:

> *OMG! DH and I just started TTC, did the BD as soon as I had an OPK+, now I'm in the 2WW and I'm sooooo nervous!! My sister had to have IVF with ICSI, and it was soooo expensive, but she has three beautiful babies so it was soooo worth it!! Do you think I should go on Clomid? This is probably TMI, but for the past couple days I've had this discharge that's kind of like rubber cement, but not really, plus a bad headache right now. Do you think I could be PG?!? Plz answer ASAP!!*

It was the era of the Octomom. I rolled my eyes and powered down the computer. Some of the advice out there conflicted anyway: Don't consult a doctor unless you've tried for six months without success. Some perfectly normal couples take two years to get pregnant. Consult a fertility specialist before you ever try. I decided to do what I do best in regards to the medical establishment: nothing. I wasn't even thirty yet. I'd find my health in our weedy garden—with a few B vitamins and folic acid thrown in for good measure.

We got down to the fun part.

* * *

Stanley and Stella started going at it as soon as the days began to lengthen. Chicken mating, a modest cloacal kiss, left me wholly unprepared for what I saw when Stanley and Stella did the deed.

Drakes are among the few birds endowed with a real penis. In a Muscovy, the organ is corkscrew shaped and can be as long as sixteen inches when unfurled from its counterclockwise spiral. They have been in an evolutionary arms race with the female ducks, who have developed clockwise reproductive tracts to stymie unwelcome suitors. As Stanley and Stella demonstrated, a drake is large enough to flatten a duck to the grass. From the amount of necking my ducks engaged in before mating, Stella seemed pleased to be made into a sex rug. Afterward, as she went off to bathe and Stanley splashed water on his back in post-coital celebration, his dangling phallus still retracting slowly, the proof of their fertility remained hidden in her unhatched eggs.

After she began to brood on the eggs, I spent too much time online trying to determine whether they would hatch and, finally, following the guidelines of a development paper from Papua New Guinea, measured the eggs during one of Stella's bathing breaks, wrapping them in a bit of white eyelet ribbon suitable for baby showers. They were large enough to be viable, a relief, but then Stella sometimes had trouble keeping the eggs warm. I'd come home from work to find she'd left the pen but couldn't figure out how to fly back in. As she marched around the enclosure whistling her concern, the eggs cooled.

* * *

After a few months of hoping for our own babies, I did take a peek at the classic *Taking Charge of Your Fertility*. A Granola

Mennonite like me can get on board with do-it-yourself fertility tracking with a combination of charts, thermometers, and divination over secretions and anatomical details. She invests in only enough ovulation prediction kits to confirm her theories. For me, everything appeared to be working well, like clockwork.

A Granola Mennonite would consider a grandmother's prayers a welcome ingredient for conception but would never tell her grandmothers, mother, or mother-in-law that she was hoping to conceive. (That wouldn't matter; they would have been praying for grandbabies since the wedding.) And she might, in a fit of mysticism, go out back to the creek, Briery Branch, to invite the spirit of her child to come from the land and the flowing water of the place, and when she found herself further downstream—say the Dry River in Bridgewater—she might fancy that her child's spirit had drifted past last month, but she would catch it here. If not here, today, then next month as the Shenandoah ran through Harpers Ferry, or later in the summer at the Chesapeake Bay, or perhaps in the fall at the Atlantic Ocean.

I eventually gave up on the spirit baby—until much later when I learned to repeat the mantra *Spirit baby in the back of the car ... spirit baby in the back of the car* while I drove, to combat one of the side effects of the fertility drugs, aggressive driving. But that would be much later. A Granola Mennonite isn't a fan of drugs of any sort, and fertility drugs sound like something for high maintenance people. A Granola Mennonite takes what comes. A Granola Mennonite finds satisfaction in her childfree life.

* * *

After all, there were ducklings in the world. After two slow days of hatching, six ducklings emerged, and Stella abandoned the nest. It was far from a perfect hatch, with quite a few unbroken eggs left. Stanley, banished from the pen, waited outside the chicken wire while Stella showed him the new brood. The scene looked like a prison visit. The babies were wobbly on their little webbed feet and collapsed quickly, taking naps under her wings.

One egg didn't have time to hatch. A little bill jabbed frantically at the shell, peeping, still trying to enlarge its window. I tucked the egg in my jacket pocket to take inside to an old incubator. The hopeful egg went quiet. Ducklings help each other hatch, peeping encouragement and sometimes pecking at the shell. I thought this one might be lonely, so I queued up the Dresden Philharmonic and duckling number seven began to sing along.

After a whole day of music, she managed to hatch: Chopin piano études, *Eine kleine Nachtmusik,* a Baroque mixed disc, twice. When the music stopped, the chick grew quiet—when I put on a new disc, she cheeped and struggled against the shell. Late in the day, she pushed off the top of the egg and flailed free. But she died by morning, a trifling thing, no more than a scrap of dandelion fluff. It was nothing to hollow a hole in the turf at the outside corner of the poultry yard, to tuck her in and fold the grass back over. Perhaps I should have followed Stella's lead. Perhaps I should have left the duckling in its shell, in the down-lined nest and the quiet darkness.

I told the story of the duckling who lived a short life of determination and music a few months later at a bonfire where friends remembered a daughter who died in her first year. Any baby takes care and love, but the ones who have the fiercest struggles—who need all we can give, who leave us in the end—change our hearts in violent ways. I was not ready for this, I thought. No one could be ready for this.

* * *

Within a couple summers, Stella had hatched dozens of ducklings, and her children and grandchildren were brooding new generations of ducks. Up to our ears in Muscovies, we butchered some and sold others each fall. True to form, I was the one who wrote the names of the ducks on the freezer bags, Jason the one who said, "no . . . please, no." With no sign of human offspring, we submitted to simple tests. It was still just a matter of weeks or months, I believed—and if there actually was any problem, it wouldn't be mine.

We both looked good. Some of our numbers weren't quite in the normal range, but no one, not even studies I found through the infallible Google Scholar, could tell us whether that mattered. We added on more vitamins, decongestants, and some dubious folk wisdom from the Internet. Eventually, I followed up on my midwife's referral for an HSG to confirm that my fallopian tubes were open. "Oh," said the technician. "You're here for the infertility work-up."

I wasn't ready to use that term. Some wicks are just slower to catch fire, I told myself while he pumped dye through my cervix. Normal fertility is sometimes defined as the ability to conceive within two years, and by that definition I still had a few months left.

"Perfectly normal," said the radiologist, showing me the dye flowing through my open tubes on the monitor.

"Where's your husband?" asked the nurse.

I stayed away from physicians for six more months, then took Jason with me to appointments. I didn't mind the duck-billed speculum, but it was nice to have a hand to hold when that long metal tenaculum clamped down inside my privates.

***

Meanwhile, this Granola Mennonite learned and grew. She taught writing. She edited an anthology about Mennonite martyrs. She planned a writing conference. She also nurtured. I taught people to walk. My grandfather, in assisted living, stumbled on his feet and wasn't allowed to leave his chair by himself, but together we could roam the halls, he with his walker, I with his wheelchair, offering encouragement. One duckling hatched with a curled foot. I worked to straighten it out. This delicate work, taping the foot of a struggling duckling to a little plastic shoe each morning, felt like grace—a new chance to save a duckling—or perhaps make a bargain with the God who watches over sparrows.

***

My mother says I was born with my legs crossed and curled, and I remember walking across an examining room while a pediatrician watched my toed-in walk. "She'll probably grow out of it," he said. "A brace is psychologically difficult." I liked this philosophy of medicine, that time is a healer, that given enough space the organism will grow beyond its disorder.

***

Most first-line treatments for unexplained infertility include ovarian stimulation, which carries with it a high risk of twins or multiples—ten to thirty percent, depending on the drugs used. To me, it was a terrifying possibility. I was no duck; one baby at a time was more than enough. When we found ourselves at last in a specialist's office, he didn't pressure me to try these procedures, but neither did he emphasize the very real risk of multiples when he laid out possible treatments.

We decided to stick with "expectant waiting"—an accepted form of treatment for unexplained infertility, but one that was waning in effectiveness as we approached the three-year mark and our monthly odds of conception kept dropping, based on population studies. We considered further diagnostic steps. The specialist suggested that I might have endometriosis. The only way to know for sure was via a laparoscopy, minor abdominal surgery, but I couldn't pick up the phone to schedule one.

* * *

The last time I tried to help with a hatch, Stella hurled herself at me, scattering ducklings, her bill lashing, and I drew back a moment too late. Her perspective on intervention was as clear as the bruise darkening on my forearm. The duckling had caught its wing in the process of hatching, and I chipped away enough of the egg that the little creature could work itself free. Stella stood protectively over him while he pushed his way out. But he remained weak and didn't survive the next day's heat wave. I resolved that forevermore, I would let hatches happen naturally for the ducks.

When they could hatch eggs, that is. One duck, Delores, kept building her nests in a rocky spot under the yucca plant. One after another, the eggs would crack, and in late summer her nest would be a stinking mess. Things didn't go perfectly for the drakes, either. Stanley's impressive phallus prolapsed and we had to separate him from the other birds for months while the long swollen end of it dried up and fell off.

* * *

All this time, many of my friends were having babies, and I attended blessingways, circles of women who offer support to the expectant mother. At each of them we introduced ourselves, naming our mothers and their mothers. It was a reminder that we were part of an unbroken line of women who gave birth. With my gathered friends I felt in touch with generations of women who were mothers and then, to my surprise, with all of the rest, the women who waited and the women who stopped waiting, or chose not to wait. There's a long tradition of them, starting with the biblical stories of Hannah and Sarah straight on down to maiden aunts of family legends, friends who carry on after a miscarriage, acquaintances without Fallopian tubes, one who tried in vitro fertilization unsuccessfully for years, one whose partner refuses to have children, some who prefer other ways to be generative.

In the bathroom at work, I chatted with a mother who dealt with infertility for years. She told me about her own surgeries and wished me well. Her embrace gave me the courage I needed to go home, pick up the phone, and finally schedule that laparoscopy.

* * *

I came home from the pre-operative appointment to find five ducklings missing from the black duck's nest. We searched the weeds all through the nursery enclosure, but feared the worst. Gray Julia sat calmly on her nest of waiting eggs. The cat yawned when I asked whether he ate the ducklings, showing off his fangs. I moved the mother and her remaining brood to a cat-proof pen. Only a few days later did I discover Julia, who should have been on her own eggs for another two weeks, wandering through the potato patch making mother-duck whistles, a handful of stolen ducklings behind her.

I apologized to the cat for doubting him and then, for simplicity's sake, returned the ducklings to their original flock. It was too late for Julia to return to her own nest. The mothering hormones were pumping and she wanted babies. She staked out a pen full of brood, thinking she might pick a few ducklings out of this larger flock, pacing the fence and whistling to them. *OMG! I found some ducklings and think they like me, do you think it would be okay to take them? Plz answer ASAP!!*

I was spared that precise sort of desperation. I never understood the attraction to babies. It was easy to be around my friends who are mothers of infants; I only grew wistful when watching older children. Actually, I Facebook- and blog-stalked a few families, really fine Granola Mennonite types with good-sized broods of kids, building treehouses and fabulous birthday cakes; I clicked through every single picture in the album of that family trip to Europe. One girl in particular stood out. With her long brown hair, she might have been mine. Simply put, I fell in love. If I hadn't, I could have stopped right there, taken what came—or didn't—like a good Granola Mennonite, waiting for the universe to call me some day and say, "Hey, you want some kids?"

Our children would not come to us freely, but I needed to meet them. I already loved them. I wasn't quite putty in the hands of the doctors, but in time I became ready to submit to needles and invest in long woolly socks to cut the chill of the stirrups. I would decide a baby was worth more than a Prius, even if they would cost the same. I would decide, eventually, that twins were a risk worth taking.

I would take it slowly, since my endometriosis turned out to be mild—a non-issue—and my eggs were in good condition. I would advocate for better insurance coverage. I would end up posting regularly on an infertility forum online. I would learn to view treatment as a right and a privilege, a justice issue, and would eventually share our story in my community, but I would still ascend the ladder of interventions one reluctant rung at a time. It would take a long while, these first awkward steps in the work of mothering, the long process of letting go.

13

The Fathers

The most terrifying thing I'll do this year is speak in front of The Fathers. Oh, I'm glad for the opportunity. It's at a *Martyrs Mirror* conference, and I'm editing an anthology of literature inspired by the book. This is a good audience on which to test my ideas about art and sacred narrative. But they'll be there, all sorts of fathers—Mennonite historians and theologians and, most nerve-racking, a large contingent of plain folk; men in suspenders and black hats, their wives in modest bonnets, embodying in their way of life my ancestors, my forefathers. I will stand behind a pulpit and talk about sacred subjects, though I will not preach. I don't know if some of the conservatives would sit for a woman preaching. Probably the mainline intellectuals will be glad to see me—oh, a young woman, taking interest in history!

All of them will notice I'm a woman, and young, too young to be anyone's mother.

* * *

I'm not typically afraid of fathers, though my own dad elicited awe and respect. He raised his voice only once in my memory, then came around to apologize to each of us individually. He worked hard so that my mother could make our home. He swept chimneys to get through computer school and later, moved in faith, without a job, so that we could live near family. He's worked for twenty years now for one company as a database administrator, at one point declining to climb the managerial ladder because he liked the work he had. He was troubled when his company took a military contract, talked to the corporate executives, didn't leave but made them think. During his long commute, he listens to World History Classics and memorizes passages from the Bible. Often, he tells us, he prays for his daughters.

I remember clipping his hair full of plastic barrettes as he lay on the living room rug doing homework after a long day sweeping chimneys. I remember the smell of soot when he came home from work, and the scent of wax and honey when he got out his beekeeping tools. I was only afraid of Dad when, wearing the horsehair gloves he used to handle firewood, he pretended to be a gorilla and chased us around the house. Do it again, we'd squeal.

* * *

An early encounter with The Fathers came when I requested a piece for my anthology from a practiced martyrologist. He's from a more conservative tradition and doesn't use email, so I wrote him a letter. He called. What was my project? Did any of the writers use vulgarities? Was this an appropriate use of the *Martyrs Mirror*? The work—I struggled to apologize for it—reflects the way readers receive the *Martyrs Mirror*, the way it is taught. What they say of the book reflects the condition of today's church.

It reflects the condition of their souls, he said.

After I caught my breath from the impact of colliding worldviews, I offered to send him a description of my project and a correspondence began. I couldn't convince him to share his work, but he didn't refuse entirely. I want his work, his perspective from his extensive travels and research. I fear he wouldn't find my project worthy.

At the *Martyrs Mirror* conference where I will present my paper, he is to be the keynote speaker.

* * *

If I had brothers, perhaps things would have been different. Perhaps our household would have been split between men's ways and women's ways, but my dad taught me to move in the world like a man. The first lesson came before a science fair. My sister and I would be talking to judges. I was painfully shy.

"Girls," said Dad. "This is how you shake hands." He explained the key elements: a firm grip, a single, confident shake, pleasant eye contact. Then he made us practice. Even today, a professional past thirty, I get compliments on my firm handshake. Girls, I suppose, are expected to have weak hands.

* * *

I tell Julia about the martyrologist in early spring, a few months before the martyr conference. Our feet are up on lawn furniture outside the Eastern Mennonite University library, where I've been searching the archives for months. Julia is a celebrated Mennonite poet, visiting campus for a reading, and she is helping me look through some of the poems I've collected for the anthology. She is strong, stylish, perhaps a bit battle-scarred, half a generation ahead of me as an academic and a fearless voice. Our skin is bare to the sun.

I'm a little worried about the conference, I confide. What if my material, or simply my presence, is too threatening? I tell her my strategy: "I guess I'll take the little sister approach."

"What do you mean?" Later, I'll wonder if she didn't sound a bit alarmed, or perhaps disappointed. Perhaps I've projected on Julia my own sense of guilt for wanting to find an easy path, sneak around through the kitchen door rather than knock proudly on the front door.

I try to explain. "Just . . . humble. 'I don't know as much as you guys, but look at the cool stuff I've found'?"

* * *

Growing up, I was good at one thing: school. At the spring academic awards program, we'd go up again and again, the smart Beachy girls without television, picking up science awards, writing awards, honor roll. At the program my freshman year, I came back to my seat after accepting my first award of the evening—stand, blush, make it to the front of the room, firm-handshake-and-eye-contact, grab the plaque, done. Dad leaned over and whispered, "Don't slink up there, or scurry. Look proud. Hold your head up. Walk slowly."

So I did, and still do, take awards graciously, though they come much less often. Because of Dad, when someone compliments me—say, after a reading—I no longer point out my errors but say instead, "Thank you. I'm glad you enjoyed it." Gracious smile. Eye contact. I do not, as some women of another generation do, apologize for the food I place on the table unless it actually is black from burning.

I don't think I've ever been told to shut up because I'm a woman. I've been encouraged to speak, rarely felt ignored. Oh, there have been employment situations and course evaluations where gender probably made an unfavorable difference—I'm not naïve about the way the world works. But it helps me, too, sometimes. And my folks never limited me; though they kept close to traditional household roles themselves, it was clearly by choice. We'd help Dad stack wood as much as we'd help Mom cook.

* * *

Researching my conference paper about artistic responses to the sacred narrative of the *Martyrs Mirror*, I spend hours talking to an author on the phone about her experience of publishing a personal essay questioning the helpfulness of the way we read the martyr stories, and the response she received from men she called "the intellectual power-brokers" of the Mennonite church. These, too, were The Fathers. I'd read the exchanges—some kind, attempting to connect on a personal level, even as they disagreed, some actually contemptuous—but all of them with a sense of supreme confidence and ownership of the stories of the *Martyrs Mirror*. "They wrote with such privilege," she said.

I don't pay a lot of attention to power and gender politics in my own community. My pastor is a woman; so is the chair of my department. The former president of Mennonite World Conference is coming in as our dean, and she shook hands, as equals, with the pope, while others kissed his ring. I feel safe.

I usually think of male privilege in an intellectual sense. I read the statistics, then write letters calling for equal pay for equal work, sign petitions asking Congress for better family leave policies, remind my students that women's rights are a recent, hard-earned innovation—even as I struggle to remember this myself, here in Obama's America. But as the conference draws closer, I feel younger by the day, more feminine, and these seem to be impediments, not advantages. In my mind, The Fathers loom in a growing crowd: some in plain coats, some with neckties, a tight band, all-knowing, all-judging.

* * *

After a family dinner, all of us gathered for Christmas or Thanksgiving—I must have been in college, or close to it—I told a joke to the assembled uncles and aunts. Walking back to the house, Dad gently noted that I stared at the tablecloth while telling my joke. "Eye contact," he reminded me. "Share your joke with them." I tried, and I still try, to do this. How difficult and distracting, to be shy. Dad wanted me to be part of the world, to not wait to speak.

A few years later in the run-up to the 2000 elections, my father and I supported different candidates. We met at my grandmother's house for my sister's graduation party, and we talked politics. That is, he tried to talk politics with me. I clammed up. I respected Dad's opinion so much, I didn't want to challenge it. "Tell me why you're voting the way you are," he urged me. "It's okay to disagree with me." He seemed genuinely distressed by my lack of argument.

* * *

I remembered that moment this week as I finished writing my conference paper. My dad gave me permission to disagree. At the *Martyrs Mirror* conference, I will enter the new room, make eye contact, have a firm hand shake, hold my head up proudly—not just for praise, but for criticism—I will face these Fathers with my dad at my back, telling me to speak up, don't be shy, why would you want to be quiet?

14

The Voice

Elizabethtown, Pennsylvania

Later, someone suggested the *Martyrs Mirror* conference would have been the perfect setting for a murder mystery. It had all the elements—the genial host, impeccable landscaping, interminable sessions with all participants crowded in a single room with wooden benches. Do you remember who slipped away while the philologist was wrestling with his Powerpoint presentation? What did the Foxe scholar hide in her handbag? How many bonnets were on the coat rack? Which kind of black hat was missing after the library tour? And that Q & A session—did you feel the pacifist tension in the air during that stand-off between the liberal scholar and the religiously conservative historian?

In the mystery, of course, the murders would mimic the torments of the Anabaptist martyrs as detailed in the *Martyrs Mirror*. After the plenary session by the conservative Mennonite historian in black, we'd discover someone bound and drowned in the lake, like Mattheus Mair. Returning to the dormitory, the chair of the Mennonite Historical Society would find a conference participant hung by his thumbs, like Gelijn Cornelis. Only a matter of time until someone would be burnt at the stake. . . .

Fittingly, I attended the conference with a residual, irrational fear of punishment. As a young mainstream Mennonite woman, I've never been discouraged from speaking or preaching, but neither had I ever stood up bare-armed (in the traditional dress of my particular type of Mennonite—sandals, etc.) and spoken before an audience that included conservatives in suspenders and beards, men who do not allow women to speak with authority in their churches.

Perhaps I feared academic punishment, too. I'd written a paper on literary responses to the *Martyrs Mirror*, and I wanted to speak to the state of the received *Martyrs Mirror* as it is read by modern Mennonites. I also wanted to make some points about Mennonite literature, and I felt distinctly under-qualified to do either. I'm a creative writer; my research and analysis doesn't usually stretch beyond my own imagination. The margins of my conference notes are a testament to my fears:

Martyrs Mirror: size stops bullets, but difficult to hide.
Martyrs Mirror: alt. to concrete shoes?

Physical violence was never a real possibility at the conference. The heirs of the sixteenth-century Anabaptists who were so brutally tortured for their stance on adult baptism now devote themselves to peaceful living. The historic violence asserts itself in schismaticism—we won't kill you for your wrong beliefs, but we'll never share the communion cup. I jotted down another phrase spoken with relish by one traditionalist presenter.

The exclusion of unworthy church members....

The night before my presentation, I went out for drinks with some congenial heretics from Bluffton. (I use the term *heretics* loosely, to differentiate folks who see movies, play cards, or go for drinks from the ones who don't and wear bonnets.) I don't like the taste of beer—so I drank coffee instead. That was my mistake, assuming my travel-weariness was so great that two cups of coffee would not keep me from sleep.

Of course it did. Lying in the guest suite at 4 a.m. beside my roommate, a gently snoring Mennonite poet, my hummingbird heart racing, I realized I would not sleep at all—at best, I could hope that a shower, or maybe a serious yoga session, probably both, would help me through the morning's presentation, that my only option for now was to lie here thinking of martyrs, reviewing my paper, waiting for the sun.

Reviewing my paper. Waiting for the sun. Thinking of martyrs.

That's when the visitation came. I was still awake, still in bed in the interminable night, the Mennonite poet aslumber, but I heard a voice distinctly, one of those aural hallucinations that usually comes just as you're falling asleep. Or maybe a *Voice,* capital *V.*

I couldn't see in the dark room, but the speaker, I felt, held out a large book to me—a Bible? The *Martyrs Mirror?*—and droned:

Do you solemnly swear or affirm ...

A culturally sensitive Voice, I noted. It knew Mennonites don't hold with oaths.

... to tell the truth
the whole truth ...

I raised my right hand and chanted along with the predictable next line:

... and nothing but the truth ...

But the speaker wasn't finished.

... and make it interesting?

I gave it a go the next morning in my presentation, yoga-stretched, freshly showered, and wholly unslept. And that is what I suppose I'll keep trying to do.

As for the conference, no one was burnt at the stake, drowned, or buried alive. No one walked out of my presentation or denounced me in the Q & A. The traditionalist gave me one of his stories for my literary collection. The historians included me in their dinner table. The poets and heretics gave me good advice. The water of the lake remained smooth and unbroken. And yet the shock of that extra, unexpected line from a Voice I thought was my own remains fresh, gives me new visions:

Do you solemnly swear or affirm to tell the truth, the whole truth, and nothing but the truth ... and make it interesting?

15

Mennonite Girls Can Read (With Recipes!)[8]

Letter to My Editor

Dear Ms. Goodrich,
　Thank you for your continued interest in my manuscript. What a wonderful idea to add a chapter of recipes to my book of essays on Mennonite theopoetics and literary history. I quite understand how that might expand the market for the essay collection. I was interested to hear your proposed title for the book: *Mennonite Girls Can Read (With Recipes!)*. My friends in marketing assure me that with a title like that, the book will sell like hotcakes. Speaking of cakes, see my new chapter of collected recipes below.
　Shalom,
　Kirsten

Aunt Jacobina's Gelächterkuchen

　Aunt Jacobina always made these tiny cakes. Of course, she wasn't really our aunt, she was the Brenneman kids' great-great-aunt, but everyone called her Aunt Jacobina. I can remember her well, with the net covering precisely pinned over the coiled mass of her long white braid. She wore her covering long after the other grandmas at church gave it up, and when we'd try to sing in unison to words projected on the wall while Brother Lucas played guitar on Wednesday nights, she would belt out an alto line, or even a tenor, because she believed we should always sing in harmony.

She was the only one at church who could make true *gelächterkuchen*. Some other ladies had easier recipes from their families, the kind you could make in one evening. Instead of baking each tiny cake in a thimble, they would just bake a big rectangle on a cookie tray and cut it into little squares. With frosting. They didn't even try to say gelächterkuchen; instead, they called them *gelach* cakes. I don't remember that anyone actually ate the inferior gelach cakes. Aunt Jacobina baked gallons of gelächterkuchen for Easter, but if you didn't get up early for the sunrise singing, you wouldn't get to church in time to taste any. After she died, I was touched and amazed to find that she had left her recipe for me, neatly copied in longhand onto a new index card. It turns out she noticed how carefully I used to dry and polish each tiny communion cup twice, there in our church kitchen after the love feast.

- 6 eggs, separated
- 3 heaping cups of flour
- fist-sized knob of butter
- pinch salt
- molasses to taste

Separate the eggs and reserve yolks, uncovered, in a cool cellar. Beat the whites by hand in a copper or glass bowl (copper is better) until stiff peaks form. Let sit, covered with cheesecloth, overnight, waking every hour or so to beat the whites thick again. At sunrise or shortly after first birdsong, combine butter, flour and salt thoroughly by treading upon it with bare feet in a small washtub. (I have found that it works just as well to rub the butter and flour together as you would for pie crust, as long as you do not wash your hands.) Retrieve egg yolks from the cellar, skim off any dust and beat vigorously. Add molasses to the yolks, but first search your soul to be sure you have no impure thoughts or worldly yearnings, or you may put in too much. Combine wet and dry ingredients, folding in the whites gently at the end. Grease and flour thimble and fill two-thirds full. Bake individual cakes one after another on the hot top of a cherry-wood-fired cookstove. (I have found that you can speed this process by purchasing an additional three or four thimbles and that an oven heated to 450 degrees works almost as well if you do not have a cookstove.) Age cakes for three weeks in a tin basket in the smokehouse or hung high in your chimney.

Groundnut and Bhati Stew

During our family's eight-year term in Arvedistan, we experienced incredible hospitality and also witnessed devastating poverty. Never did we feel this more strongly than in our first year as we toured a remote mountain region and came upon a family of nomads suffering the effects of a decade of drought. Their cattle were all gone and they had climbed into the mountains to harvest groundnuts, a back-breaking process that required the help of everyone in the family from the ancient grandmother down to the scrawny son who had never seen rain in his lifetime. Outside their tent was tied a well-mannered little animal, something between a goat, a wildebeest and a toy poodle in size and appearance. The boy explained through our translator that this was a bhati he had snared here in the mountains. It was quite tame, and he showed us how he had trained it to open the hide flap of the tent.

The family insisted that we come inside and we sat on the dirt around a smoky fire while the patriarch of the family hosted us in the rich tradition of a four-hour long tea ceremony. When he explained they had no yak butter to add to the tea, we were able to offer the butter we had brought in our packs as a gift. Later, the grandmother brought in an aromatic stew and the son began to weep. We asked the translator what was the matter and he explained that the child was weeping with happiness because he had been able to provide meat for their honored guests. The family insisted that we eat and sat about laughing and clapping delightedly as we ate every last drop of the stew.

Later, we were to learn from a visiting conservationist that our bhati meal was rare indeed. The last recorded sighting of a bhati was back in 1989, so this was the last known living specimen. This knowledge only increased our humility at the gift we had been given. Not only had that child on the brink of starvation given up his pet for us, but an entire species had given its all to make us feel welcome. I have done my best to recreate the recipe for the stew by substituting inexpensive ingredients you are likely to have in your kitchen, but to really experience it, you must spend an eight-year term in Arvedistan taking lessons in humility.

- one chicken, cut up (or, if you can get it, goat meat, cubed)
- 2 Tbsp. margarine
- medium onion, diced
- 1/4 tsp. garlic powder (optional-spicy!)
- 4 Tbsp. peanut butter
- tomato juice
- salt and pepper to taste

Heat skillet on medium-high. Melt margarine and fry onion until soft. Then brown the pieces of meat on all sides. Add garlic powder (if desired) and peanut butter; cook for a few more minutes. Cover with tomato juice and simmer until meat is cooked through and very soft, about one hour. Season with salt and pepper to taste. Serve on rice. For special occasions, top with slices of hard-boiled egg.

Forget-About-It Salmon Pot

What I love about slow cookers is that you can bless your family (and yourself) with a hot, home-cooked meal, even after a long, hard day. There's nothing like coming home to a pot of goodness after hours talking sternly to customers who try to take more than three garments into the dressing rooms at the Mennonite Central Committee thrift store, or driving the kids around town (from soccer practice to Bible quizzes to the math tutor to Simplicity Club), or typing frantically to keep your Mennonite food blog up-to-date and witty so that the publishers will notice you. What a relief to see that your dinner has cooked itself! I love slow cookers so much that I often have four of them simmering at once: one for main dish, one for dessert, one for side, and one for salad.

This recipe is especially good for church potlucks. The other day, I went to a potluck at the Baptist church and it was downright dismal. Take-out chicken, store-bought pies, seventeen different potato dishes, and not a single green vegetable. (Okay, so I went back for seconds, but I had to go on a juice fast for the next week to make up for it.) I was glad to get back to my own church. I just have to say it: Mennonite churches have the best potlucks ever! We have ethnic foods and healthy foods, and there's always someone who looks out for the vegetarians and brings lentils. Sometimes it's hard to keep up with the Millers and Tiessens and Yoders and all their fabulous food, but don't worry! This unique dish restored my position at the front of the pack. I have had many, many requests for the recipe, so here it is. As usual, I have included a couple of wicked little secrets to make sure people will be scraping the bottom of your slow cooker and asking for more.

- 2 cans wild Atlantic salmon, drained
- 1 cup jasmine rice, uncooked
- 1 cup Gorgonzola, crumbled
- 1/2 cup dried apricots, finely chopped
- 1/2 cup walnuts
- 1/8 cup cilantro, finely chopped
- 2 cloves garlic, smashed
- generous sploosh of balsamic vinegar
- freshly ground pepper to taste
- broth to cover

Combine in slow cooker and cook on low for 6-8 hours or on high for 3-4 hours.

Wicked little secrets:
- You can substitute any blue cheese for the Gorgonzola. But be sure to use full-fat cheese in all of your recipes. No one keeps track of calories at a potluck.
- Lightly toast the walnuts in a skillet or toaster oven before you add them to the pot.
- You don't actually have to pick the skin and bones out of canned salmon before you use it. I did this for years before I realized that they just disappear during the cooking—poof, like magic!

Fresh Local Garden Salad

As we become more aware of the ways that burning fossil fuels does violence to our Mother Earth and her community of creatures, we look closer to home for food sources. Making your own salad (with a little help from the Great Creator) takes a little more planning, but the rewards are great and go much deeper than flavor.

Double dig a patch of earth to sustainably clear it. Amend the soil with some of your compost, but only if you have been careful to separate out the meat and citrus peels. If not, bury your compost and start a new bin for next year. Meanwhile, stir some well-aged manure into your garden patch. (We have found that several local businesses have hitching posts for Amish customers, so I keep a large bucket in the passenger's seat of my car to collect any "fertilizer" I may find in the parking lots.) Plant a diverse mixture of leafy greens from seeds you have saved from last year's garden. Using seeds produced by a corporate interest defeats the purpose of this recipe and will make the salad bitter.

Allow the good Earth to feed and water your salad garden. Do not weed this patch. Remember that many of the plants we in our agro-centricity call "weeds" are wholesome foods. Purslane has a sweet tang, lambs-quarters is as nutritious as spinach, and stinging nettles are rich in protein.

To serve, roll out sustainably harvested bamboo mats around the garden patch when the leaves of the greens are 6-8" high. Advise your guests to lower themselves carefully onto the mats, so as not to compact the soil. It is better to lie down than to sit, as this distributes your weight more naturally (and makes up somewhat for the excessive bulk that most Americans carry about these days).

Gently pinch off the tips of the greens and enjoy. Be sure that you do not use scissors to snip them, as this damages the plant. For best results, don't even use your fingers—just graze. No dressing is necessary—the savor of sunshine and self-righteousness should make this salad go down easily.

Blessing for the Meal

Now thank we all our God, with forks and spoons uplifted,
for butter and for meat, and flours lightly sifted,
that we are Mennonite, and mean to stay that way,
that food is love, and we have plenty for today.

16

Walking

Briery Branch, Virginia

Celeste's right foot was curled into a tight fist, so she staggered about on the back of her wrist. Hot weather during her hatch may have made her foot webbing stick together, and a few days with a hitch in her waddle cemented the deformity. Ducklings grow fast. I feared her joints would mature permanently askew.

Her first shoe, a skeleton of match-sticks and Band-Aid scraps, failed at the touch of her flailing foot. I finally managed to unfurl her webbing against a tiny shoe cut from cereal box cardboard. She dissolved the shoe in the water pan, but I had a working model.

* * *

My grandfather's shoes are black and barge-like, with tired Velcro flaps. He'll tell you they're good shoes, two hundred dollar shoes. Neuropathy keeps him from feeling his feet and puts him at risk of falling. When he steps, it's by sight and memory, not by feel.

His feet are large and wide to the fourth E, with a massive big toe he's passed along to all of us. He can put the shoes on himself, he says, but he lets me do it; it's faster. I smooth the Velcro straps flat, and they curl back up, fuzzing at their ends.

* * *

Nobody could tell me how to shoe a duck, though a few members of Internet poultry forums suggested tape, toothpicks, and stiff cardboard. Full-grown ducks who lose feet in accidents, those that don't become soup, seem to end up wearing baby sneakers. One crook-footed duck in the U.K. wears a wood and leather shoe; his keeper laces him into it each morning.

Celeste was always last in the line of Muscovy ducklings fleeing the nest box when I raised the lid. Her wild, mohawked sire huffs like a steam-engine when you approach him, and he wrestles lesser drakes into submission with his powerful neck and massive wingspan. Celeste fought with all of the same spirit, but she couldn't escape. My hands engulfed her yellow body.

To shoe a duckling: Cut plastic from the lid of a salad greens box to the size of the duckling's foot. (At first, this will be smaller than a dime.) Hold the duckling by the ankle, gently but firmly. Focus only on the foot. Ignore everything that the duckling tries—whether she flails, flings her tiny body about, peeps shrilly, or snabbles at you with an outraged beak, hold her ankle steady. Hook her claws around the outside edges of the plastic shoe, gently sandwiching shoe and foot between thumb and forefinger. With the other hand, fix a tiny strip of surgical tape to her toe and wrap it under the shoe. Repeat with a thistledown touch. Don't tear the webbing of her foot. Don't squeeze the duckling. Use flesh-colored tape to camouflage the duckling's shoe; her mother tugs at the white kind until it pulls free.

***

In his new room in the Mennonite nursing home room, Grandpa isn't allowed to stand by himself. He used to hurl himself out of his chair and plow across the carpet on his wheeled walker, taking calculated risks. Now, if he pulls a stunt like that, his chair alarm rings. Instead, he pushes his call bell and waits for someone to come for him. He wants them to take the alarm away, but the shrill cushion on his wheelchair is standard issue for his floor.

I learn how to help him transfer from his wheelchair and shepherd him while he walks with his walker. He knows the litany and repeats it for me and his therapist: Set the brakes. Scoot to the front of the chair. Lean forward, nose over toes. Balance your hands evenly on the walker and hoist yourself up. His therapist shows me how to follow, the wheelchair in one hand,

Grandpa's belt in the other, ready at each moment to tip him into the chair if he should lose his balance.

***

I changed Celeste's shoe in our back hallway, where we track in mud and hang our coats. It was easy to clean her droppings from the linoleum. I kept a box with scissors, adhesive, and plastic scraps in the hall for our morning sessions. Morning after morning, for the twenty or thirty minutes it took, I shod and unshod the duckling, uncertain whether we'd made any real progress.

Certainly her toes were straighter, but they could barely flex; as soon as I removed the shoe, she lurched about on the back of her wrist, her now-flat toes trailing like an unfurled fan behind her. Sometimes, she'd try walking on the side of her foot, but the phalanges on the edge of her foot crumpled under her full weight.

With the shoe on, she was agile enough. She stumped around on the tip of it, like a ballet dancer en pointe. Without it, she slipped and slithered, splaying on the linoleum, until she found purchase for her claws in the floor mat. As soon as the new shoe was secure, she hobbled ably to the back door and cheeped for her flockmates. She still struggled when I worked on her foot, but she didn't have a mortal dread of me, and if she skittered down the hall away from me, she also came hitching back.

***

From the vantage of his new room, my grandfather is amazed by the labyrinth of halls that connect his facility to the rest of the retirement center. The new arrangements mystify him. He tries to explain: "My room is here, but if you go way out down the wing and around by the Wellness Center, it's there, too."

It's hard to tell at first if he is confused or joking. Or confused and joking about his confusion.

Grandpa walks the halls every chance he gets; he usually wheedles a CNA into walking him to dinner. His knees and elbows sometimes hurt. Tylenol and topical cream help. His therapist tells him: if it hurts, don't do it. But he loves to walk.

For our first walks, we take a simple lap through the halls around the courtyard, but one day Grandpa suggests we go to the auditorium. He claims to know the way, so we set off, my fingers hooked into his belt, my other hand pushing his chair between us. He lists a bit to the right, so I tell him to stand straight.

"One thing Libby does, she gives me lots of encouragement," says Grandpa.

"Good job!" I tell him, "You're doing great!" He declares that he has earned a break. He rests in the wheelchair at an intersection of hallways but hasn't forgotten he's taking me to the auditorium. Wherever that may be. When he heaves himself up again, he points his walker down a hall that leads out of the wing.

Through the code-locked door, around a corner and up a ramp, there's the auditorium. Grandpa beams, glad to find it right where he remembered it.

* * *

Ducks don't do well alone, so the day I took a risk with Celeste's shoe, I returned her to the flock as usual. I changed the balance of the shoe by padding the end of the plastic so that she'd be forced to tip her toes up. I wasn't sure that the straps would hold, or that her ligaments could handle the new strain, but nothing else could break her habit of hobbling en pointe.

Unlike my chickens, who fight over food scraps, the ducks are social creatures; they pass each other tasty bits and work together to pull them apart. If one duckling in the yellow nap-time pile picks up a twig, the flockmates will pass the twig from bill to bill until every duckling has examined it. They help each other hatch. If left alone, they die.

So Celeste went back into the pen, experimental shoe and all, as much as I would have liked to keep her inside for observation. The next morning, I went out early to see how her foot was faring with the treatment. I found, as usual, the remains of the orthopedic shoe near the water pan. A clutch of flat-footed yellow ducklings hustled away, so Celeste must be hiding in the nest box. I hoped not nursing a broken foot.

But no one was in the box. One of the yellows had to be Celeste, flat-footed as the rest of them.

***

Grandpa has plenty of visitors: friends and family members who also live in the retirement village, church people, me. He plays in the chime choir, joined the Old Spice club, even tried an art class. He's hung his walls with family pictures and has a tractor on his bureau to remind him of his farming days. My aunt brought him a planter full of forest plants and soil from the woods around his family's cabin. His out-of-state children call more frequently these days.

His wife, my grandmother, walks down from their old independent living apartment to see him every day. But it's not the same, he tells me, not after you've lived with someone for over sixty years.

He knows that his walking won't get appreciably better, that the most he can hope for is to maintain his abilities, but I think he also wishes he could get up and walk, without setting off any alarms, down the hall, past the Wellness Center, through the corridors of the complex to the apartment where Grandma still percolates coffee in the morning, hums over her paints and threads, and reads in the lamplight.

***

For a few weeks, I could pick out Celeste by her pigeon-toed walk, but even that straightened as her white feathers grew in. She could be any one of three sleek sisters, perching and preening together. Many of our young Muscovies end up on our table, but I wanted Celeste to enjoy her hard-earned flat foot. We found friends who wanted some egg-laying ducks and traded Celeste and her family for sausage, seed garlic, walnuts, and a heart-nut tree.

Grandpa tells me about the dream he had just after he moved into nursing care. He was floating without his walker, without the wheelchair. "I was dying," he says, "but I was allowed to stay to say goodbye." He floated all around the home, up and down the halls. He saw us all. It felt wonderful.

***

Some mornings, white feathers flash past my window—young ducks, flying loops around the house.

17

C is for Clomid

A. ADOPTION

The man at our church probably means well when he jokes that the quickest way to conceive is to adopt. After all, the evidence stands in the front every Sunday—our pastor who became pregnant with twins shortly after she had adopted her son. When people tell you that you should *just adopt* to break the conception logjam, you must decide. You can 1) educate: "Well, actually, studies that control for all variables find that adoption actually depresses conception rates!" or 2) pick a catchphrase: "Why don't I just save time and adopt twins?" or, better, "Go to Hell."

B. BABIES

Maybe you don't even like babies, have never been interested in the larval state of the human being—at best, warm little bread loaves, at worst, squalling poop factories. The desire to procreate isn't, for all of us, about that elusive newborn smell. (One friend swears it's like cookies; the other is rhapsodic about the buttered popcorn scent of her baby's diapers.) It does nothing for me. I do think a chubby baby looks delicious. I may have considered the proper herbs for seasoning one. Dear reader, I understand if you think I might not be fit for motherhood.

C. CLOMID

But if, like me, you nevertheless want a baby, your doctor will probably start you on Clomid. The nurses may warn you about "Clomicidal" rage. Of all the pills and creams and suppositories and injections that may be in your future, this little one may throw you off the most. You are likely to run off the road going too fast around the curves, even if you have respected the speed limit in the past. You will get in touch with anger you didn't even know you had. You will develop paranoid terrors of tractor trailers crushing you.

D. DEAR HUSBAND

Jason drives us to the fertility clinic. He is my DH: what we call husbands on the fertility message boards. It's almost all moms on the boards, and our DHs are recurring topics. Maybe DH doesn't even want kids, or to spend any more money, or isn't tuned into the heartbreak of miscarriage. Maybe DH copes by staying at work later every night. If your DH does not have good toilet seat etiquette, be sure to record this in the forums. My DH is a good driver. I keep my eyes closed on the interstate.

E. EXPECTANT WAITING

Before I started Clomid, we practiced what the British call "expectant waiting" to manage our unexplained infertility. It took three years to accept that no baby would come, no matter how carefully I charted my temperatures, monitored my fluids, and timed the encounter that the forum ladies called the BD—the Baby Dance. Oh, there was still a chance, each year, a few percentage points, that expectant waiting would result in a baby. But do the math: stack up a few points per year in your remaining supposedly fertile years. See? The odds are not in your favor.

F. FERTILEBOOK

On the infertility forums, we call Facebook "Fertilebook." Our pregnant friends don't know that most of us block their updates. We don't want to know that their fetus is the size of a cherry, a plum, a pineapple. Instead, we are busy TTC, obsessively using our OPKs, charting the timing for our BD with our DH, hoping for a BFP but positive we'll get a BFN. We shower each other with babydust. We enroll in the roll call for this month's IUI treatments and stalk the roll call for last month's IVF treatments. Lots more BFPs over there.

G. GAMETES

If you have money, you have options—you can start with options. If you want to replace DH's genetics with those of a catalog donor (*advanced degree, high I.Q., athlete, musical talent*) or arrange to have a daughter to go with the pink nursery you've designed, buy the gametes you want. Pick your embryo. DH and I still root for a child with our own genetic idiosyncrasies: definitely nearsighted, on the introverted anxious side, with the fat Yoder big toe and massive Alderfer jaw. Either way, if your gametes aren't coming together, you'll have to start saving up.

H. HYSTEROSALPINGOGRAM

The radiologist who administered the hysterosalpingogram after a year of waiting was the first one to use the word: "You're here for an *infertility* workup?" Nope. Just ruling things out. Was he disappointed later, after he injected the radioactive dye and watched it flow freely on the monitor? My fallopian tubes were as good as anyone's—good as the tubes of the twenty-something assistant who held my hand during the procedure. DH was at work. No big deal, right? Infertility is for salted fields and some other kind of woman, a high-maintenance woman. Not for me, not for you.

I. INSURANCE

Too many twin pregnancies pop up on the forum—let's call it Infertilebook. Twins increase the risk of C-section and postnatal intensive care. Insurance covers the hospital costs, though. Funny they pay for those hundreds of thousands in the U.S. but won't cover the procedure we all want to have, the single transfer in vitro fertilization with low risk of multiples. With a limited budget, your best bet is to pay for Clomid and intrauterine insemination, hoping that double egg production and washed sperm will do the trick—or to inject gonadotropins and pray for no more than triplets.

J. THE FAMILY JEWELS

Men rank their virility by the numbers—inches of penis, how many babies they fathered on their wives, millions of motile sperm. After each IUI, the doctors tell DH, "Good job!" as if he has any control over his swimmers. Even if there are no known issues on the sperm front, your DH will want to feel he is helping. Don't deny him reasonable purchases of vitamins and herbal supplements. Let him switch from briefs to boxers, or put a lead apron on his lap to work on his laptop, or eat figs daily, if he wants.

K. KIDS

Did I say I don't much care for babies? Kids make me wistful, though—all those quick, small-boned humans whose parents post photos of them on Fertilebook building gingerbread lighthouses, sporting shampoo bubble hair-styles, rescuing baby squirrels, climbing onto porch roofs. I don't block these albums—I bookmark them. I stock my shelves with children's books. I plan family vacations, scheme up elaborate road trips through the national parks system. Don't deny it—you have the names picked out, too. On holidays, while you're chopping celery in the kitchen, you can hear them whispering around the piano in the living room.

L. LADY PARTS

Do you ever envision your baby girl, born with the incubator of the species already tucked inside her? The burden of procreation will rest on her. If problems arise, even if her partner participates in treatments, she will be the one who must unfold her lady parts monthly to the technicians and the waiting universe. Her DH, if she has one, will make his donation in private. Knowing what you know, would you prefer to have a girl or a boy? (Either one, as long as it's healthy, you say? We'll save that conversation for another day.)

M. MENSTRUATION

Even if your daughter grows up fertile, she will worry when her period is early or late, if it is too heavy or too light, or if it arrives at an inconvenient time, and she will worry when it dwindles into menopause. This child must learn to ride her cycle, and you can teach her much more than the other mamas about this, those seven out of eight who have coasted from menarche to menopause without having to stop and patch the tires, rethread the chain, or call a specialist. You'd be a good mom for a girl.

N. NEGATIVE

BFN—Big Fat Negative—sometimes, that's the entirety of a woman's post to Infertilebook. There are more BFNs than BFPs, with just enough positives to keep us coming back for more. You can check out the threads for the next levels of intervention—in vitro, donors, surrogates. The steps, if we can find the money to take them, are clearly laid out in cyberspace. But off the message boards, we're on our own. Out here, infertility is a joke with a simple punch line—"just relax!"—rather than a widespread and treatable medical condition that ought to be covered by insurance.

O. OVULATION PREDICTOR KIT

You'll need to buy an Ovulation Predictor Kit for the treatments. Brace yourself. This is not going to be an anonymous process. Once, I went through three different Wal-Mart cashiers to find one in Customer Service who was authorized to open the plastic box in which they had imprisoned the OPK. Apparently, it was a high-theft item and in such demand that only a few Wal-Mart employees could be entrusted with the key that opened the box. "Good luck," said the lady who finally rang me up. Be prepared to respond to inquiries and unprofessional well-wishers.

P. PREGNANT SILENCE

Perfect the ability to hold a charged silence when people ask rude questions or try to give unsolicited advice: "Just get really drunk—it worked for us!" or "Clearly you have unresolved issues with your mother and your womb won't open until you cleanse and find closure." You might follow Miss Manners' advice for dealing with unwelcome inquisitors. Ask, "I beg your pardon?" in tones of mild dismay, as if you must have misheard. If they persist, raise your chin a half-inch and repeat, in more fervent tones, "I beg your pardon?" Repeat as many times as necessary.

Q. QUITTING

You might log in to Infertilebook one day to find whole threads on quitting. FingersXed is quitting smoking. Egg Queen is quitting Pilates because she is afraid of dislodging an embryo. Praying247 has run out of money and she is really quitting treatments for good, this time, although she has said it before. She says she is never coming back. Too much money, too much heartbreak. If these treatments don't work out, I'll quit when I go back to teaching in the fall. I'll quit Clomid and save money for IVF, adoption, or a fabulous, heart-breaking, childfree life.

R. RABBITS

You might be one to start a blog about infertility, or Instagram your injections. They're out there, the comedians and the performance artists and the careful, serious gatherers of resources—helping each other, sharing their journeys in public. I started a blog anonymously, speaking as my aspirational spirit animal, the rabbit. I posted twice, one of the posts a long rant about the way department stores hold ovulation predictor kits hostage. Then I gave up. There's no creative energy in the moment. Maybe later, from notes, when I've resolved it one way or another, I'll be able to write about it.

S. SPERM

Obsessively purchase your DH bottles of Vitamin E, zinc, and selenium, even if his counts are fine. It normally takes tens of millions of healthy sperm to have a chance at fertilizing an egg, and the overall quality of sperm in the human species is degenerating at an alarming pace. Most of them are corrupt from the start; they have two tails, or giant heads, or can only swim in circles. Some men manufacture sperm with so many heads that they look like chrysanthemums. Extinction via poor sperm could side-swipe our species like a tractor trailer. Supplement accordingly.

T. TENACULUM

Once, I let a midwife at the local practice perform an insemination. She couldn't get a good angle on my cervix and pulled a tenaculum on me. A tenaculum is a long, cold pair of tongs with barbed hooks in the end. Another time, a specialist amid a procedure said, "Looks like we're going to have to get out Mr. Tenaculum." Maybe I misheard his words—I was too shocked to beg his pardon. Wearing fabulous socks will improve morale while you're in the stirrups, but cutesy names won't make the tenaculum friendlier. Valium might help.

U. URINE CUP

I keep a red plastic 12-ounce cup under the sink with a big, black "P" markered on it. This is my pee cup, washed and stored for the two weeks between the ovulation prediction strips and the pregnancy test. I hum "Red Solo Cup" while filling it, just to break the tension. Why don't I just throw out the cup each month and get a new, definitely not contaminated one, you ask? I don't know exactly why. P cup is my companion. We're comfortable. I want P Cup to get lucky one of these months, just like me.

V. VESSEL

A woman is a vessel, a container, a ship. She is meant to set sail, to go forth bearing. She is defined by an emptiness that can carry something growing. But this empty hold, this zero space, isn't static. Zero can grow bigger. Zero, repeated, can become the biggest number there is. Each morning the digital stick registers "Not Pregnant," sigh or cry or curse, hand it off to your DH, and ready yourself for the next round. The future, which could have been a brisk current pulling you forward, will dissolve into the flat water of doldrums.

W. WEEPING

The Infertilebook ladies write about crying all the time, but it isn't my style; I'll just eat sea salt caramel chocolates, maybe brew some raspberry tea for uterine support, and log in to the support forum to register my BFN on the July IUI roll call. We all keep up faithfully with the roll call, and you should, too; it's bad luck not to. When you post your BFN, Egg Queen will probably ignore your post in her eagerness to report early pregnancy symptoms. FingersXed will type, "Shit!" Praying247 will shower you and all innocent bystanders with babydust.

X. X-ACTO KNIFE

I find DH at the kitchen table, dissecting the digital pregnancy test with an X-acto knife. The kit contains a basic urine strip with a single blue control line, next to a test line that also turns blue if it detects pregnancy hormones. Tiny lights inside the device illuminate the strip, and an electronic brain interprets the results and reports them on the screen for the human user— apparently to spare us the difficulty of counting two lines. He shows me the battery reserved for this single, disposable use, plus an inexplicable tablet the size of an aspirin.

Y. YOGA

After chocolate, I usually try some yoga. *Tadasana*. Mountain pose. *Vrksasana*. Tree pose. *Natarajasana*. The Dancer.

143 Martyrs and Chickens

Tonight, I will interrupt my yoga to see why Jason is still in the kitchen and will find him with the guts of the pregnancy test still spread about him, coloring the test strip with a blue felt-tip pen, trying to trick the digital brain into saying "Pregnant." He will be too intent on the project to notice me standing in the doorway, so I will tiptoe back to the yoga mat and sink into the next poses. *Sarvasana.* Corpse. *Garbhasana.* Fetus.

Z. ZYGOTE

The test is 95 percent accurate, and I believe the negative verdict. If a zygote was made, and if it had properly implanted, my body would be full of its hormonal messages. But after dark, you might feel that there *is* an embryo, a boneless ball of cells floating there, its signals not quite loud enough, its hooks and wires not quite strong enough to burrow into your uterine lining. In the dark, it is okay to plead with it, quietly, so that your DH, spooned up behind you, won't hear: *Stick, baby. Stick. This time, please stick.*

18

Lavish Banquets

Used to be, Monday nights, you'd double-check your list of discussion questions for tomorrow's workshop. Now you grind oatmeal for cookies. Students are perpetually hungry. They are in delicate transitional states; something is dying, something is being born. Their freedoms still fit them ill. You woke to it gradually: the young woman who confided the truth behind the doctor's notes, long after you guessed that "heart trouble" was a euphemism; the one who didn't confide anything, who remained thin and drawn and silent all semester, and didn't return the next, and you wish you had said something, had known what to say; the heedless young men tearing their hair over the missed conference time, the online quiz. And then there are the ones half-crazed with new philosophy, faint with enthusiasm, up all night with extracurricular reading, painting protest signs. Someone needs to feed them.

Audit a poetry course, the first time you've sat with the students in years. Your own students are classmates, now, and poetry is not your native language. You write 80 Works in 14 Weeks; that's the name of the course. You love it, the uncertainty and challenge of it all. The professor feeds you the first evening—sourdough bread with homemade butter—and soon everyone is signing up to bring snacks. Sated with berry scones and lemon bars and buckets of coffee you read your poems, and your mouths are primed to feed on the words as a feast.

But of course. When you meet with your writers' group, it's always with food. Wine makes you generous with your critique, your confessions. Tea helps you feel safe. And the cream puffs? They tell you that someone loves you very much.

Food is love. You've heard that in the context of overeating, or the way to a man's heart. It's true, though, the most primal form of connection. For mammals, it's how we learn to be alive, the nourishment we suckle from our parents.

Go home to your mother when hip surgery puts her in bed. Follow her specific demands each morning: Stir the fiber drink made with a teaspoon of powder (a regular teaspoon, not a measuring spoon) and serve it with a chaser of prune juice. Brew a cup of decaf coffee grounds with a teaspoon (a real measuring spoon, not a regular teaspoon) of caffeinated grounds added. Split the sprouted wheat muffin for the toaster and top one side with a free-range egg, fried, the other with fresh-ground peanut butter. Follow a tyranny of specifics from the half slice of pepper-jack cheese for the egg to the number of raisins that garnish the peanut butter.

This is the most important thing you'll do all day, beyond changing the bandage and disinfecting the twenty-seven staples, beyond squeezing her feet into compression socks or waking in the night to help her to the bathroom. She must wait six weeks while the bone knits to ceramic and chromium, and she will have breakfast the way she wants it.

At the nursing home, your grandfather will serve you iced tea made from mint he's grown in his garden box. Now that he can grow turnips and tomatoes, he feels more at home. With the tea, he becomes a host in his semi-private room, one wall a curtain.

Last year in the hospital, gripped by the infection that brought him to the nursing home, he wouldn't take any drinks from the attendants. Only the cup in your hands was safe; only the water you brought him was free of poison.

One old man at a church potluck asks if there will be eating in heaven. Eternal feasting, you want to say. Remind him of the scroll Ezekiel ate in his vision, etched on both sides with words of lament but sweet to his tongue and filling to his stomach.

You can't take food to all of your students, but you make it part of the weekly workshop with the newspaper staff. Baking is your lesson prep. While you stir the dough, consider what nutritive feedback they need this week. Try to combine decadence and nourishment: oatmeal and duck eggs in the cookies. Fatty dip for the carrots.

Something shifts when you eat together. You see them more clearly. You talk more easily. The physical exchange mirrors what's happening underneath, an intellectual exchange, but all of you are more comfortable with the etiquette of eating. This is what I brought today, you say, and they take it up gladly and thank you, naturally. How rare to bring a lesson on Associated Press style with such free and generous joy; how much more rare for students to return thanks for it.

Search an academic database for "pedagogy" and "feed students." Find that people spoon-feed students, feed students' fears, feed students grades, feed students a preset, standardized curriculum, feed students into the academic camp, the high school, the university. No one in the journals just feeds students, period. There's something unprofessional, unexplored, too feminine, wild, when you acknowledge your students' stomachs. A student is a mind.

Know better. Preheat the oven to 350 degrees.

19

Honey

Briery Branch

My husband is crossing the meadow with honey in his hands. How beautiful, how sensuous: *husband, meadow, honey, hands,* as bright as digging potatoes at dusk with him, moist earth under my feet, is dark. He forks as I scrabble with a three-pronged trowel, and we sort through the dirt together. The light is so dim we find the potatoes by feel. He hands them to me.

How hard it must be to have a marriage in the boxed apartments of the city. I try to remember what gifts we gave each other in Morgantown, substitutes for the first ripe tomato, hands full of blackberries, news of ducklings, of bee trees, of rain.

My husband is crossing the meadow with honey in his hands for me. He jogs so that the bees he has brushed from this hive frame won't track him. I meet him in the middle, take the frame of wax-capped honey to add to my box of bee-free frames. The sun shines through the matrix of honey, golden. Pooh-bear honey, Jason calls this color. Some frames are paler summer honey, some a deep rich spring honey. All of it glows.

On the page, this morning, the honey in my husband's hands is so bright, so luminous, I have to remind myself of something earthly. I look to the disorderly back hallway, the gallon jars to sterilize so we may fill them with honey tonight, the sticky evening of extracting ahead, the possibility that today the bees will find a way under the duct tape-sealed truck topper and into the honey supers, boxed and bagged and weighted down though they may be, and steal most of it back.

Jason will come home from work early tonight, and we will spend the evening spinning the frames to extract honey, and when we are finally finished, our skins will be sweet with honey but we will be too weary to make love.

The honey extractor and other equipment we will use tonight belonged to a man just a few weeks dead. Our bee mentor, Sandy, took his final flight to the other side but taught us what he knew about honeybees before he went.

How I love the things of this earth; I am overwhelmed by its abundance. In a week of rain, the cucumbers erupted from their patch; I stack them like wood on the front porch. The first tomatoes are climbing up the front steps, onions spilling from their mesh bag, heavy ropes of garlic hanging in the kitchen.

Jason's leaving for a week, taking a trip to Nebraska to meet distant family, to fill in some gaps in his history. Before he goes, he gives me a birthday present, a pressure canner. I told him what I wanted, reminded him of my birthday amid his packing. Long past are the days when I'd wait for him to remember, make him guess. We know how to ask for what we want.

I can jars of pickles while he packs, but there are cucumbers to spare and more on the way. I will give them away, throw them to the chickens, turn them into compost to surprise us next year with cucumber shoots.

You don't have to pick every fruit from the vine, I remind myself.

Leave some for later, Jason says whenever he tears himself away from a mountain view.

I won't weep in my husband's absence. I'll finish my book. I'll can tomatoes and beans, catch up with reading, my girlfriends, review textbooks.

But when he comes home, we'll eat honey and fresh bread, finish digging the potato patch, make our plans for the fall, for next year, for the next.

Life won't always follow our plans, and sometimes we won't even be able to agree on a plan. We'll weather new troubles together and separately—we don't yet know how lonely, angry, or overwhelmed we will be, how even after years of marriage, we'll stumble around each other speaking different languages. And yet, a long time from now, as long as memory glimmers, perhaps long after Jason dies, I will still see him crossing the meadow with honey in his hands.

20

Written On I

At a Mennonite/s Writing conference in 2012, a spring where the Shenandoah Valley bloomed early to welcome the visiting writers, and where I coordinated all of the local logistics, poet Jean Janzen, who taught poetry in one of my college classes, asked me what I was writing these days.

I was somewhere in a long, slow season of low-level unsuccessful treatments for infertility, a year away from starting serious IVF treatments. I was an underemployed adjunct professor, a few months away, though I didn't yet know it, from landing a continuing contract as an academic administrator. I was subclinically depressed—maybe clinically, but no one was asking. I wasn't working on anything.

I gave her what felt like a clever, throwaway reply. "Sometimes you're writing. Sometimes, you're being written on."

Now, years later, as I gather my separate essays together in the hope of forming a memoir, I find wide gaps in the telling, especially in the most recent decade, incomplete arcs in the manuscript, events I have not recorded in journals or essays.

This non-writing busyness, my full-time employment, no children, helped to pay off our debts in one short decade, gave us the privilege of pursuing more aggressive treatments for infertility—expensive in this country, routine healthcare in others. I was writing, sure—writing curriculum, mission statements, and quality enhancement plans. The job and the treatments left me with little energy to record what came, but it is recorded in body and memory, indelible snapshots.

***

In summer 2012, the Beachys gather for a reunion in southern Indiana—Grandpa Claude and Grandma Edna, six children, a mass of grandchildren all grown up, none of them small anymore. There's only one great-grand, and he's too young to travel, so we make much of my cousin Heidi's kitten. The Beachys are famous for highly scheduled reunions, from the meal plan to who washes the dishes with whom to the proper order for family sharing. Schedules are posted, and there's always an appointed timekeeper for the sharing time.

During the sharing, my sister and I both reveal that our families are dealing with infertility. We find ourselves perched together on a giant hassock, with the entire family gathered around, laying their hands on our heads and shoulders, the family sharing stopwatch paused, for once.

"Open their wombs, O Lord," my uncle intones. We try not to peek at each other. We try not to giggle.

***

Two cupcakes, brave in pink and topped with a dried cranberry each. The left one has a proud banner stuck into it with a toothpick: "Good luck, Lefty!" I decorate them for Elaine the night before her single mastectomy in 2009. We don't know whether to laugh or cry. The next day we find out the cancer made it into her lymph nodes—not all of them, but some. Bad news, but not the worst. There will be chemo, and then seven good years of remission.

***

I'm alone, in a chilly guestroom, preparing to self-inject my first round of IVF drugs, the slimmest of needles into the softest part of my belly, a job that Jason trained to do. But Harold is in the hospital following cardiac arrest, which he miraculously survived by virtue of already being in the hospital for a minor heart attack. One minute, he was sitting up chatting with one of his many friends on the phone, joking about his ambulance ride from his doctor's office, the next moment, he was on the floor, red-lining.

Then followed many days on life-support, the black eye from his fall swelling and changing colors, Elaine and Jason and

I rotating between the guestroom of family friends and the intensive care unit, while I drove the hour home to meet shipments from the specialty pharmacy, kept my medications on ice, kept to the hour-by-hour schedule for injections and treatments for my growing cluster of eggs, in preparation for extraction. Alone in the guest room, everything in my body fights against sticking a needle into myself—I close my eyes, grit my teeth—and feel almost nothing as it slides easily under my skin.

* * *

Alone again on the balcony of a retreat lodge in the mountains where I'm leading a student writing retreat, looking out over the trees, the valley below, and the mountains beyond, I take the call from the clinic. The IVF nurse is pleased. The number of viable embryos growing in the medium typically decreases in the days following extraction, but our number somehow has increased, with some borderline eggs thriving unexpectedly. We have good candidates. I squeal on the phone to Jason. It's hard to contain my excitement as I return to dinner with the students.

* * *

I cannot self-inject the progesterone shots that come later, after a first unsuccessful embryo transfer and the one that follows it. These fat shots go directly into the gluteus maximus, daily, for months. Fortunately, Jason and—a few times—my sister can wield the needle for me. It's a thick, oily medication that needs to be warmed and injected slowly, over several seconds. Never particularly patriotic, I find that for some reason humming "The Star-Spangled Banner" is the best way to relax my body and free my mind in these moments. Obama is president. *Yes we can.*

* * *

I'm not superstitious, but . . .
1. In spring 2013, we find a bird nesting alongside our house—one of the Muscovies, deep under the azalea beside the basement steps. A bird nesting on your house is a sign that a baby will come, but we've had Muscovies nesting in one corner or another for years with no results for the humans in residence. What's interesting is that this

spring we find a second Muscovy nesting by the front porch, this one tucked under the Alberta Spruce.
2. My friend Carrie has a blessingway, a gathering of women to celebrate the new life she will bring into the world. Melody, friend and midwife, is there. She nudges me and tells me to take a small cowrie shell from the heap on our little altar. "They're a sign of fertility," she whispers. I take two home with me.
3. I drive to Atlanta to spend a few days with my sister. She attends the kind of church where the preacher asks everyone with a birthday that month to stand and pray for the wishes of their heart. What the heck, I stand with the rest of the July birthday people. They pass me the mic. I'm nervous. I mean to say I want a baby, but what I actually say is, "I'd like some babies."

* * *

I'm in my car in a parking lot somewhere, talking on the phone with the IVF nurse. The results from my blood test are in. It's very early, but the numbers indicate that I'm pregnant. Extremely pregnant. I know from the fertility message boards that this is twin territory, possibly higher. On the second round, after the single-embryo transfer didn't take, we did transfer two embryos at once, per our treatment contract. I ask the nurse, a bit timidly, about the odds of triplets.

"Oh," she says reassuringly, "There's only a ten percent chance that an embryo will split in IVF."

I know how stats work. The numbers suggest both original embryos took. And if there's a ten percent chance that one has spawned a triplet, that also means a 10 percent chance the other has spawned a triplet, which means a 20 percent total chance of triplets and a 1 percent chance they're now quadruplets. (The literature will show that the nurse and I are wrong about these odds, but in the moment, they are stunning.) I take in a long breath.

* * *

The numbers continue to rise steadily. At the first ultrasound, our doctor introduces us to the pulsing clusters that will be Baby A and Baby B.

"No Baby C?" asks Jason. The doctor shakes her head. We let out the breaths we've been holding.

* * *

An upset stomach is a sign of a healthy pregnancy, so altogether it's a good thing that I'm huddled here by the toilet on the bathmat in the hotel room in Nebraska, waiting to see if my stomach will settle. I pass the time by checking email on my phone. There's an unexpected note from the man who came out this spring to buy our muscovy chicks, after those nests under the azalea and the Alberta spruce hatched out nineteen ducklings. He wonders if we'd like a little Dexter cow, a middle-aged loner who doesn't get along with his herd. "If you can find a way to pick her up she is yours for free for the kindness you have shown me."

We're already adding twins to our menagerie. What's an extra cow, more or less? We'll take her.

* * *

Elaine always imagined having lots of children. She tells us her dream family had a pair of twins in it, identical girls she could dress alike. But only Jason came, only after years of waiting, and when she awoke after the Cesarean, she learned that the doctors had taken her uterus.

* * *

In November, before the doctors ground me from further air travel, I fly out to visit my grandmother Beachy, who is in failing health. The babies are four months along, just starting to stir. We expect grandma still has a few more weeks or months, but within three days, she'll be gone. For now, though, she is well enough to sit up on the couch beside me and the main attraction—my belly. Grandma Beachy wears size two shoes and barely reaches my shoulder, but those small hands are firm on my stomach. We both hold our breaths, hoping for a touch, listening with our bodies. And then—two strong kicks, and a few wriggles. The babies put on a show for her.

"Boys or girls?" she asks. It's secret so far, known only to me and Jason.

I lean over and whisper in her ear.

Her eyes brighten.

She takes our little secret to the grave with her, even though her daughters try to get her to spill the beans.

Her final words are, "Every breath is a gift from God."

* * *

It's late in the day when they finally discharge me and the twins from the hospital, because there are so many tiny details before they'll release us, we're new to the intricacies of five-point hitch baby seats and snappy pajamas, and I can barely hobble along as it is. It's snowing in earnest now as Jason drives slowly, because the snow is a little unexpected here on the last day of winter, and the roads are undertreated, and it's a relief when we finally turn into the driveway at Briery Branch and see the smoke rising from our chimney.

Elaine and Aunt Loretta have been waiting all afternoon for us and the twins, keeping the soup warm. They usher us in, unbundle the babies from their seats, then nestle them into the old Alderfer cradle in the warm living room. It's the cradle where Jason's great-grandmother Katie Freed rocked her children. There's a heart cut out of the headboard, which was broken and mended with a couple of metal braces, and the cradle is long enough to hold two babies, one at each end of the new mattress Elaine made.

* * *

Later on, while there's still snow on the ground, I'll creep outside and build two tiny snow girls on the picnic table, give them stick arms and baby sunhats and eyes from the tiny dried-up fruits of the Bradford pear trees.

* * *

Not many weeks later, I'll carry Irene outside to feel the sunshine on her face for the first time, as April breezes shower blossoms down from the pear branches.

* * *

In another eye's blink, six years later, Irene will shake those same branches to make the petals fall so that Sallie can dance in the pretend snow, while Irene shouts, "Now is the time to take a picture!"

21

Notes from the Night Owl Feed

Briery Branch, Virginia

Second Breakfast
Irene: Left + two oz bottle
Sallie: Right 20 diligent minutes
Pump: skipped

It's breakfast again. I get organized in the nursing rocker that Aunt Loretta brought us. It has no arms, which makes it easy to position the tandem nursing pillow and adjust the strap around my ever-evolving waist. The rocking armchair from Aunt Jewel, just across the living room, is better for actually rocking Irene when she screams all evening.

I tuck a folded flannel blanket into Sallie's side of the pillow to catch the drips and ready the nipple shield for Irene. "Baby me!" I order Jason, and he scoops his oldest daughter out of the cradle where she has been fussing and hands her to me. I tuck Irene under my arm, and she burrows toward my nipple. I have only seconds to help her get a good latch before her angry head-shaking starts and she knocks off the shield. This time, we're lucky. She clamps on, and my milk flows quickly. I won't have to syringe milk under the shield to keep her interest.

Jason brings Sallie, and I add another shield and nudge her into place, hoping not to dislodge Irene. With her low muscle tone, she needs back support and a finger under her chin to reinforce her latch. She's wide awake for once, and chomps away with more interest than expertise. Some of the milk is going down her throat, I think.

Jason waits with a back-up bottle in the battered recliner where I have been sleeping. It hurts to lie down post-Caesarean. When Aunt Mim comes to help, she will buy us yet another rocking chair, a big leather recliner, and we will squeeze it into this little room alongside the cradle, the bassinet, the woodstove, the couch, the armchair, and the two other rockers.

* * *

Lunch
Irene: Right +1
Sallie: +2 oz
Pump: 2.5

Sallie is working hard at her bottle, trying to hold it all together—the suck, the swallow. Milk drips out around her tongue. She'll manage a couple of ounces. In the bassinet beside me, Irene awakens and stretches, a mighty stretch with one arm back and the other forward, like a warrior, an archer. In a moment, she will start to roar. She is fierce and wonderful. My gaze falls back to Sallie's small face, her limp arms, her elfin ear. She is soft and vulnerable.

My lion. My lamb.

I bought the palm-sized wire bound notebook weeks before their birth, planning to record my improvised notes on breastfeeding times, pumping, and supplemental bottle feeds. I printed out charts to hang above the changing table where we could keep a tally of diaper changes and drew a diagram of where all the baby clothes belonged. There's even a little note clarifying which diaper balm is compatible with our cloth diapers. On the refrigerator are lists for household helpers. My calendar has different aunts, grandmothers, sisters, and cousins scheduled to stay with us for a full three months. Our church family signed up to bring us meals three times a week for three months. I stocked up on toothpaste and detergent to last for months. I thought I was fully prepared.

I was not prepared for Sallie's diagnosis.

Neither was the girls' doctor in the hospital, a kindly country doctor we had chosen because we didn't want to drive twenty minutes into town for all their appointments. He didn't disclose his suspicions about Down syndrome until two days after they were born, not until Jason urged him to explain Sallie's low muscle tone.

At the girls' first check-up, the doctor's partner cheerfully presented the possibility that Sallie might not have Down syndrome. Sure, her eyes had the classic epicanthal folds, but he thought her face looked a lot like Jason's. It took us a month to find a competent pediatrician and have her diagnosis confirmed via genetic testing, a simple blood test we could have had at the hospital, had we known, had anyone offered.

* * *

The Feed of Milk and Cookies
Irene: Left? nursing all the time! So much spit up.
Sallie: Right +3 oz
Pump: 4 oz

It is bad form to get crumbs in the babies' hair. However, I eat most of my meals and snacks over their heads because they are always nursing, and I am always hungry. Irene doesn't seem to mind the bits of sugar cookie raining down, so long as the milk keeps flowing.

My sister sent me a novelty cookie card. One sugar cookie looks like a chick, the other like an egg. The card is welcome right now. My sugar cravings amp up in the afternoon.

Coming from her, the card is especially poignant. She is amid IVF, and it hasn't been going well. I remember our own experience: the years of low-grade depression—years when time had little meaning for us, each year like the one before except for the increasing aggressiveness of treatment. It seemed like everyone we knew was having children, maturing to the next stage of life, aging naturally. In the mirror, I looked more like a teenager every day. I felt like one. I didn't like it.

When we finally conceived twins via IVF, I was slightly ashamed to fit a stereotype so closely. It felt intemperate to end up with more than one baby. We tried to avoid it, opting for single embryo transfers as long as our contract permitted. To be fair, when we agreed to transfer two embryos, I rooted for both to thrive. My heart quickly wrote new terms of motherhood.

We made it through treatments because I loved my baby for years before she was actually conceived. After two years of infertility, I saw an eleven-year-old girl in a play. She had long brown hair like me, was coltish and self-confident. Driving home in the dark, I knew I would have a daughter like her. I loved her already, enough for all the medications to be injected, the miles to be driven, the dollars to be spent. Years later she arrived, one of two embryos.

I did not see a girl with disabilities and intuit that I would someday be mother to a child like her. Now I must wait to find out who Sallie will be. My heart must revise those terms of motherhood yet again.

***

The Sunset Feed
(tandem)
Irene: Left
Sallie: Right +3 oz
Pump: 4 oz

And now it's getting dark. After this round of pumping, I need to give the pump parts a real washing. Tonight, other people are managing Irene while she screams herself to sleep. Sallie fell asleep at the breast and is peaceful in her bassinet. The pump and I have come to an understanding. I sit and rest while it sings to me. Usually the lyrics are simple:

broccoli, broccoli, broccoli, broccoli.

Or

lollipop, lollipop, lollipop, lollipop, lollipop

Sometimes they are encouraging:

pump lady! pump lady! pump lady! pump lady!

And sometimes the pump philosophizes:

the more you pump, the more you pump, the more you pump, the more you pump

It's almost dark by the time I finish soaking and scrubbing the pump parts. With newborn twins, you develop a new relationship with time. There's the impossible math of breastfeeding one child with a high palate (try to latch thirty minutes, feed at least ten minutes) and another with poor muscle tone (twenty-five minutes), following with a supplemental bottle for both (as long as it takes for each), then pumping milk (ten minutes) and repeating the process again three hours after you started, which is right about when you finish. Day and night cease to have meaning. All times are in this armchair, with this one or that one, napping when possible, in an almost hallucinatory state, opened eyes and closed eyes meaning more than light or dark outside the window.

I used to sleep through every night. I could barely make it through a day on less than eight hours of sleep.

* * *

The Glow Worm Feed
Irene: Right? +1 oz
Sallie: Left +2 oz
Pump: 4 oz

When I'm most fatigued, there is only room in my mind for the most immediate tasks: where is the nipple shield? I found it on the ground earlier and did something with it. I'm so tired. Maybe Sallie will take the nipple bare this time. If I can make it through this feeding, maybe I can skip the start of the next one and leave a bottle for my mother to feed the next baby to wake. I'm covered with milk from a spill during the last pumping. I need to change my shirt. The sash from my sweater coat is missing somewhere. I try to get into the bathroom, but it's locked. I pound on the door. No one is in there. They are all in bed until the next feed. My hands are clutching, shaking. My mom does this all the time, locks the door on one side and exits through the other one. Irene is getting too dependent on the bottle. I don't think she needs it at all anymore. I ought to give her the breast at the next feeding. I tear every cushion off the couch. No nipple shield.

Finally, it turns up on a tray of pump parts. Who put it there? I get the baby latched on, feed her. Swaddle her. Hand her off. The other one. Stumble to the old recliner to sleep.

The house is too full. Jason, the girls. The breast pump. Rotating relatives.

There were eight people in our little room at the hospital, watching while I tried and tried to get Irene to latch, while she screamed, while the lactation consultant soothed. Nurses, relatives, all standing up and craning to get a better look. I told them all to go: *Everybody, get out!*

What on earth will I do when they go?

* * *

The Night Owl Feed
Irene: Some nursing on Right
Sallie: +3 oz
Pump: 4.5

Even when I fall into deep sleep, I'm aware of the babies, alert to their first cry. Or rather, to Irene's. She's the one I see and hear in my dreams. She's the one I look for when I wake. Sallie needed bottle feeding more, so others tended her while I held Irene. Sallie is everyone's baby, but I don't really feel that she's mine, not yet. I love Irene passionately and—when she screams for colicky hours—desperately. I love Sallie dutifully.

When she grows up and asks about her babyhood, will I confess?

I heard you stirring many nights, but I didn't pick you up or feed you because I knew you wouldn't cry. I fed you last, always, because I knew you would wait until Irene finished. I said to others that this was the gift that you gave us, the way we were able to manage infant twins, but my heart said I was taking advantage of your more passive nature. It wasn't a gift; you were the limb I was gnawing off to survive.

But tonight, Sallie wakes and calls out, a crabbed little shout. My still-shrinking uterus cramps with the rush of hormones. I do recognize her, after all. She's learning to fuss, and I will learn to be her mother.

* * *

The Feed of Wee Terrors
Irene: Right side-lying giant spit up!
Sallie: +2.5 oz
Pump: 4.5

Sometimes when I'm pumping alone in the dark, the pump's songs take a sinister turn:

you pump blood, you pump blood, you pump blood, you pump blood

Or the paranoid:
they are coming, they are coming, they are coming, they are coming

I wonder what will happen when I am alone with the girls at last, when our helpers leave. So far, there's no time or solitude for deeper neuroses to take root. I've read with interested horror about postpartum psychosis, the rare cases where women go truly mad—some enough to harm their children, to drive them off bridges and drown them in bathtubs. I read about the attorney who strapped her infant son into a baby carrier and jumped with him off a building. She was morbidly convinced he had suffered brain damage from bumping his head on the carpet and decided to commit double suicide rather than live with a child suffering from a defect. The baby survived the seven-story fall, cushioned by her broken body, although she did not.

I know what form my madness will take, if I ever snap. It will be in the kitchen, the most dangerous room of the house. The new microwave is big enough for a baby. I hide from myself the knowledge of where I keep the hunting knife we use for butchering Muscovy ducks. It horrifies me, but recipes do float into my mind: a simple roast with carrots and potatoes, rosemary and thyme. Irene is fat and tender like a little rabbit, just the right size for the small roaster.

Of course I wouldn't do such a thing, although I do nibble on her darling toes every day in play. I have heard that of the few women who do develop serious postpartum psychoses, only a minute percentage ever hurt their children. But we all have our ideations. Even my grandmother admitted to having the impulse to chuck her crying baby out the open window.

I never imagine eating Sallie.

* * *

Sunrise
Tandem, sequential
Irene: short & sweet, passed out
Sallie: Right?
Pump: 4-5 @ 11ish

I dream that we decide to give Irene away to a friend who is infertile. Jason and I walk through the Rockingham County fairgrounds, the site of our annual Mennonite Relief Sale, on our way to bestow her on our friend, but I begin to feel concerned. How could I give up Irene after all? I tell Jason we shouldn't do it. "You should have thought of that earlier," he says. He isn't swayed. It's a relief to wake with the sun in my eyes, knowing that we can keep her. But two still feels like an embarrassing wealth of babies.

The March morning Irene and Sallie were born, I caught a glimpse of each one during the Caesarean, but then began to feel the obstetrician at work and got knocked out with general anesthesia for the rest of the operation. I truly awoke to the girls a half hour later that morning, my vision doubled as I tried to reconcile what appeared to be two clocks on the wall enough to see whether I had missed a crucial window for establishing nursing. There were two babies, but when my doulas turned back into one doula and the clock resolved into one clock, two distinctly different babies remained.

And then night and day blurred together into the babies' hunger, time floating on an endless stream of milk.

But someday soon, about the three-month mark, time will hook me like a fish and drag me forward, accelerating beyond anything I've experienced. I will find it difficult to snap Irene's yellow romper, the one with the red flowers and the gather in the back that makes her look like a wizened little woman when I sit her up on my lap for a burp. I will realize that it is time to put the romper away, that before a few more moments pass, she'll grow right through the six-month clothes and the 2Ts and be in women's eights, towering over me, pitying me for my old-fashioned values, packing her suitcase, out the door, globe-trotting, leaving a great silence in the house.

For a mother coming off three months of evening colic, the prospect of silence should be a considerable relief. But I will panic. The house of my heart has grown new rooms. The twins belong here with us.

I will panic, and then I will be comforted. We have Sallie, too. Sallie, who is just learning to smile, who shouts for joy to see us in the mornings, whose disability or loyalty may keep her at home with us, or at least nearby. With this child, I must let go of my generic aspirations for her, let her define contentment her own way. Nobody knows who she will be or how her potential will change as the world changes. But if she ends up staying close to home, that will be fine with me. And I owe it to Irene to hold her future as lightly as I am learning to hold Sallie's.

I hold them both. I let them go.

22

To the (Unattributed) Mennonite Pastor who Said that Children are for Martyrdom

Dear Sir—or shall I address you as Brother in the tradition of North American Mennonites in the earlier half of the twentieth century? Brother, then.

Brother Pastor, it came to my attention that you said something shocking in an ecumenical gathering of pastors. To be fair, the word came to me third-hand, in a Facebook posting from a friend who'd read the article where you, a Mennonite pastor, were cited answering the question *What are children for?*

"That's easy," you said. "Our children are for martyrdom."

I hope, Sir Brother Pastor, that you don't have any children of your own.

Let me begin again. I am a mother, and I persisted through five years of infertility to become one. I'm a baptized Mennonite, properly baptized at the age of confession—if that is what you can call my awkward adolescence. To reassure you that I am Mennonite by pedigree as well as confession, my people are Yoders and Beachys, dairy farmers and missionaries descended from Pennsylvania Amish and Mennonites, and before that from those who fled religious persecution in Germany and Switzerland—those who did not stay to become martyrs but sought a new life. I am part of a congregation that claims the name *Mennonite* as you do. I meet with them some Sundays on Zoom while folding the week's laundry, and some Sundays in person in our rented space at a high school, overflowing with young children and agnostics and activists and professors and retired pastors who come to Shalom for the informal atmosphere and the progressive theology.

When the twins were born, these people—my people, our Mennonite people—saved us, body and sanity.

Exhibit A: The Birth Announcement

With joy, Jason and I welcomed sisters into the world, Irene Beachy Alderfer and Sallie Beachy Alderfer at 6:34 and 6:35 on Thursday morning via C-Section. Irene weighed 6 lbs 9 oz, Sallie 6 lbs, 1 oz, and we are so happy they got to grow for a full 39 weeks.

The twins are not a matched set! Irene is alert and full of energy. She has busy hands and likes to nurse but gets impatient and fusses (a LOT). Sallie is quiet and snuggly and works hard to nurse but is getting the hang of it. Our doctor noticed on Friday that she has some characteristic features of Down Syndrome, which is likely to be part of our family's story. We are just beginning to learn what this may mean for all of us. We are busy, tired, grateful for good support from friends, family, and medical staff, and so very much in love with our girls. Please join us in our prayers of "Help," "Thanks," and "Wow!"

Body and Sanity

When we announced the birth of our twins to the congregation, my friend and congregational meal coordinator wrote back, "You have a community that is eager to help and love. You will never be alone." All spring, our people dropped by to welcome both babies. They congratulated us, instinctively knowing they didn't need to offer condolences that one girl was born with an extra chromosome. They shared stories and encouragement,

helped us find a better pediatrician and, most of all, they fed us—
three months of meals, double the usual, since we had twins.

I wrote down everything our Mennonites brought into the
house:

> Chicken casserole, salad, fruit, sesame cookies. Chicken
> broccoli casserole. Salad. Muffins. Honey baked carrots. Soup, bread, salad. Quiche, cookies, fruit. Coconut
> lentil soup, salad, good bread. Tuscan bean soup.
> Breakfast casserole, salad, quinoa bread, Cadbury
> eggs. Rice and peanut sauce. Pickled beets. Fruit salad.
> Cookies. Quiche, asparagus, grapes. Spanish soup and
> cornbread. Pesto, salad, fruit, bread, cookies. Tortilla
> soup, corn bread, chocolate. Beans and corn bread.

In the first weeks, family stayed with us to help with the relentless feeding schedule—nursing and pumping and bottle-feeding each baby.

> Chicken, potato filling, roasted cauliflower, strawberries, raspberry pie. Praram tofu, spicy tofu, Broccoli
> Sesame Chicken. Lamb, salad. Potato casserole, peas.
> Lemon coconut cake. Rice, beans, chicken, tortillas, watermelon. Potato salad, asparagus, baked oatmeal.
> Muffins. Venison barbeque and nettle rolls.

By May, I was alone with the twins on some days. Jason emailed from work: "Prepare your tastebuds for sweet potato bisque, kale salad, multigrain bread, and rhubarb buttermilk cake, thanks to Ann."

I replied, "Yum! All three of us have been sitting on the couch crying."

> Chicken casserole. Wonderful curry. Chicken noodle
> soup, salad, bread, rhubarb goodie. Spaghetti casserole. Soup, bread, delicious cookies. Pot of soup, decadent chocolate cake. Coleslaw, cookies, meat loaf,
> casserole. Coconut shrimp soup. Casserole. Banana
> chocolate cake. Dumpster diving soup. Pizza.

By June, the girls were fat, thriving, and social. We scheduled the baby blessing. My parents came in from Indiana. The Alderfers came up from Louisa County, Elaine bringing with her two long white dresses that she had sewed—christening gowns, really. (Yes, we know that Mennonites don't christen. Maybe she was inspired by the enormous, lacy gown worn by Prince George at his christening earlier that year.) The twins' gowns were edged in lace and came with matching bonnets. Together with us, Shalom congregation prayed a blessing over the babies, then sang while we carried them around the room, and everyone reached out to pat a fat fist or touch the trailing edge of a gown.

Part of the blessing we use at Shalom comes from Ursula K. Le Guin's "Initiation Song from the Finder's Lodge," and it enjoins our children to walk through life with care, mindfulness, and courage—and to be sure to come back to us. Back, presumably, to these Mennonite roots.

Nursing healthy growing twins, I ate in a desperate haze of hunger and sleep-deprivation. For almost six months, every cell of human matter the girls gained came straight out of my body—and most of that nutrition arrived at our door in our church's casserole dishes, canning jars, and repurposed yogurt containers. They supported me and my body in growing the bodies of these children. In a material way, we belong—soul and body—to Shalom, which in turn is part of a larger body of Mennonites.

Brother Pastor, have you given your body to grow life in this way?

I knew from the start that most twins come early, that there wasn't much I could control. But I could do protein. I ate so many Body Builder Clif bars, mozzarella cheese sticks, sardines and eggs. Jason tried to help, sneaking lentils into baked oatmeal. I ate, and we grew, and I ate, and this body stretched beyond all believing, and by the end, I weighed half again what I weighed at the start of my pregnancy. This body carried the twins to term and did its darndest to labor them out. This body, please allow me, kicks ass.

By the time they were three, this body returned to the size it was before twins. People regard these transformations as if they are something that the mother controls or aspires to, as if she has done a good deed, if she drops the baby weight. Please understand; there was no time to exercise. I did not diet. I forgot, most days, any bodies except for the two small ones demanding incessant care. There is no virtue or vice, only me, this body, doing her work. Before IVF, I couldn't make babies, again through no virtue or fault. I am probably still infertile.

In the months of recovery, weird things happened to this body: I grew a mysterious and massive knob of flesh on the end of my finger. Lumps and bumps formed under my skin, and strange pains against my lungs prevented me from lying down. Eventually a mass on my liver was found to be the remains of a post-surgery infection, with nothing left but sacrificial white blood cells. At random, a subcutaneous gap opened where my C-section incision had healed, and I dressed the gap twice a day for months, packing ribbon through a hole in my skin in stolen minutes in the bathroom, the only ten minutes of the day when I could be alone. The official opinions regarding each one of these developments, from a variety of medical professionals who responded with skeptical looks and then careful examinations, were simply: "Ewwwww!"

Don't get me started on the IVF that made me a mother. How do you feel about needles?

Brother Pastor, I hope you have, at least, delivered a casserole.

You know that our church as a whole is not always the best on bodies, fracturing over what kind of bodies you're allowed to love. My midwife is a woman, married to a woman. She leads music at my church, and if we had to choose between broader church affiliation and her, there would be no choice at all. Years ago, one of our pastors sacrificed her credentials for this. We switched church conferences. We're sticking with our people.

I hope you'll acknowledge that the institutions of our church have not protected women's and children's bodies or their voices. Shalom does its best, with inclusive practices, with Safe Congregation policies, with socially active and trying-to-be woke members; but still, not every body feels immediately at home, stepping or rolling into our predominantly white gathering in a meeting space that meets the regulations for accessibility but may not always be accessible.

Mennonite mythology, you know, hinges on martyrdom and unspeakable violence to the body, commemorated in the book *Martyrs Mirror*. I'm sure you've studied the intricate engravings by Jan Luykens. Which one lingers for you? The image of Leonard Bernkop, tied to a stake as the flames rise higher? Maria of Monjou, standing at the edge of the dock, barefoot and bareheaded while the executioner ties her legs for drowning? Or the sword falling on Wolfgang Binder's neck while the blood spurts out? My personal favorite, if you can call it that, is an image of the sons of Maekyn Wens sifting the warm ashes where their mother was burned in a public square in Antwerp, seeking a trace of her to remember. They eventually found, and preserved, the metal screw forced onto her tongue to prevent her testimony.

You might be surprised to know that Jason and I asked for, and received, a copy of the book for our wedding. (I wouldn't be surprised to hear that you did, too.) It's enormous, like an old-fashioned church Bible, and is not fit for the eyes of young children, although it would make an excellent booster seat, and I have used it to press ferns. I'm keeping *Martyrs Mirror* with its fascinating torture pictures and embedded assumptions of moral superiority locked up in my office for the time being. It's an odd collection for a peace church to keep as a sacred text, don't you think? Yet in his recent social history of *Martyrs Mirror* (you must have read it), David Weaver-Zercher asks whether Anabaptists could have sustained their commitment to nonviolence for half a millennium without the stories of their martyrs. These stories are part of who we have become, even if I can't see how to carry them with grace.

Let me tell you about small shoes[9]

The genes on Sallie's extra twenty-first chromosome interact with the genes on all her other chromosomes, tinkering with her entire body's programming. And yet, somehow, Sallie's body is compatible with life. She has two dimples on her left cheek. One of her ears folds like an elf ear. Her teeth came in late, like sharp little posts, and her bite can draw blood. Every muscle in her body is soft. Her body is made for snuggling, but defying gravity is an effort, and she is exhausted at the end of a day. She can breathe, she can grow, she can feed herself and take off her shoes and even talk, despite the mouth that's a bit too small for her tongue. When crawling took strength she didn't have, she invented a little scootch and propelled herself around the floor on her bottom for months. When you come into the room, she can light up like a birthday cake and breathe a delighted, "Hi!"

Irene knew what language was for almost immediately. She babbled with speech-like sounds on the changing table. At four months old, she used the word *cup* correctly, in context, twice. She called me "Mama!" for the first time on August 15, Assumption Day, which celebrates Mary the Mother of Christ, and although Mennonites don't go in for Mary much, I do, and I thanked the blessed mother that my children would not be babies forever. By two, Irene was light on her feet, a quick climber, hanging off the top of the rocking chair when she thought I wasn't looking, asking herself reprovingly, "Are you being safe, Irene?"

My mismatched twins reminded me that we live in strange and precious, remarkably flawed, miraculously functional, ultimately terminal bodies.

I walked into their room one afternoon to see Irene napping in her new twin bed, cheek on the pillow, knees tucked under, rump in the air. All I could see was Alan Kurdi, three years old like her, one of many Syrian children drowned on the dangerous passage between Turkey and Kos in 2015, photographed at the water's edge in the same pose, as if asleep, still wearing his small shoes. His father Abdullah stood in the room beside me, pleading. *Change their world.*

I learned all over again how to read the news. Every child drowned, lost, injured, left in a car, bereft of medical care, orphaned by bombs, or torn from their parents becomes a particular child. My own. In the weeks and months after the twins were born, I thought often, *I could not flee, even alone, in this body right now. How far would we get? Better to stay where we are, and die together in our home.* And later, as I gained strength, I thought, *What if I could only carry one? Who would I choose to leave behind, or send to safety?*

Of all the shocking images in *Martyrs Mirror*, the one that troubles me the most is the engraving of Anneken Jans handing off her fifteen-month-old son to be raised by strangers on her way to execution by drowning. I try, but fail, to imagine what intense combination of personal conviction, external oppression, and religious interpretation might lead me to leave my daughters so unprotected.

(If you're worried about young Isaiah, please know, as Anneken could not, that he was adopted by a baker with six children and grew up to become the mayor of Rotterdam. He did not, however, become a Mennonite.)

I wonder what you thought when they found the bodies.

They found the bodies of the UN investigators in an unmarked grave on March 27, 2017. One of the peace workers, MJ Sharp, went to the Mennonite university I attended and where I currently teach. He arrived a couple years after me, a friend of my younger friends, cheerful and easy in his body. I didn't know him well, but I was proud when his work in Congo was featured in NPR interviews; he was one of ours, doing what he could for the world. Working for a church organization and then for the UN, he'd go out into the bush, deep into rebel territory, where he would sit under the banana trees with rebel leaders to share stories and convince them to think of their children's futures, to lay down their arms so the children could go to school. Some did. More than 1600 left the jungle and returned home because of his team's work. He was changing the world.

In the aftermath of MJ's murder, a friend shared an article from *The Other Journal*, a 2004 interview with Christian ethicist Amy Laura Hall about the purpose of children. Hall related this anecdote: A Mennonite pastor is asked, "What are children for?"

"Our children are for martyrdom," he says.

Hall said, "At that point, I was thinking, 'That's why you're a Mennonite and I'm not.'"

173 Martyrs and Chickens

And this is where you come into this story, Brother Pastor. I don't know who you are, although I tried, without success, to contact Hall to learn your identity. You said what you said years before MJ was killed. It might not be fair for me to predict how you would respond to his death, but I think you would put him on a pedestal, the realization of all of your hopes for our children.

I have heard of Mennonite youth ministers who pass around replicas of the sixteenth-century tongue screw. Are you one of them? Did you ask the Mennonite teens in your congregation, "Could you do it? Could you hold fast for your faith? What are you willing to die for?"

These questions were in MJ's mind. His biographer Marshall King, in the book *Disarmed* (2022), relates that a young MJ once stood at the riverside site of martyr Feliz Manz's execution by drowning and said, "Wow, I wonder if I could do that?"

During the World Wars, Mennonite leaders emphasized the stories of our martyrs to offset the popular imagery of soldiers serving their countries, trying to help their young men to believe that conscientious objection was as heroic an option as military service. MJ's father, John, told the *Goshen News*, "I have said on more than one occasion that we peacemakers should be willing to risk our lives as those who join the military do. Now it's no longer theory."

This is a moving and pertinent sentiment, but I am a mother. This is not why we feed our children so well—we are not fattening them up for either martyrdom or military service. Shalom's baby blessing says *be fearless*. It also says, *be careful, be mindful*. It says, *be always coming home*. Veneration does not bring MJ back. This earth would be better if he still walked on it.

My colleague Kimberly Schmidt shared in a 2018 sermon, "Run Dirk, Run!" how our church's use of martyr narratives compounded her difficulties in an abusive relationship. You've seen Dirk Willems featured on the cover of *Martyrs Mirror*. As this Dutch Anabaptist fled imprisonment across the ice, his pursuer fell through, and Willems turned back and rescue him. As a result, he was recaptured and burned at the stake. Schmidt explained that "As an abused wife, I could not be helped by Willems. I needed an alternate narrative, one that pushed me across that frozen river and shouted at me to keep running." In her sermon, she shared the tales of Helena Von Freyburg, a wiley woman who fled the authorities various times, set up congregations in three different places, sometimes submitted, fled when she needed to, kept working for the cause, and died peacefully of old age. When I tell the twins the story of Dirk Willems someday, I will also tell them of Helena Von Freyburg. I want them to know that it's okay to run, that a woman need not always turn the other cheek.

Menno Simons himself is remembered as a bit of a trickster character, escaping potential capture by misleading the authorities. Like Helena von Freyburg, the founder of the Mennonite branch of Anabaptism died peacefully of old age and, as legend has it, was buried in his garden among his cabbages.

MJ's friends remember him as a prankster: he filled his high school with mice and once rewired the bell system so that he could make it ring at random times, perplexing administrators for months. His trickster humor and ingenuity served him many times in his work, defusing many tense confrontations, and I only wish that he had been able to talk his way out of trouble on that March day in 2017. We still don't know for sure who wanted him dead and what purpose his assassination was supposed to serve.

One thing I know: martyrdom was never the goal, even as MJ joked that if he died in his work, it would at least draw international attention to the troubles of the region. I wish he had lived to pursue his original plan to return to the United States and live with his friends, find ways to carry and honor the trauma he had witnessed in Congo, perhaps continue the work in new ways. I wish he could go gray with the rest of us, hold children on his knees, make them go wide-eyed with stories of his narrow escapes.

In a post at "Radical Discipleship," (2017), Sarah Thompson and Tim Nafziger wrote after MJ's death, "The wider church can honor a peacemaker that has been killed not by putting them on a pedestal, and distancing ourselves from the pain of loss, but rather letting it enter us."

MJ wanted to come home. It's true that he was brilliant at his work and salvaged the futures of hundreds, maybe thousands of families through some of the peace deals he helped to broker. And yet he knew he needed rest, a break, sanctuary in time from the great pain of the world. He was planning to return to the U.S. to join an intentional community, in part so that he could do contemplative inner work. Thompson wrote, "He never got that chance, but I still do." And as she left her position at CPT, she carved out time for rest, healing, and contemplation.

Another friend of MJ, Amanda Gross, challenged readers of a post (2017) on her blog "Mistress Syndrome" to consider what conflicts and opportunities for difficult work we may be avoiding here at home as we venerate the death of a peacemaker in a far-flung location.

> Rather than see MJ's journey as exceptional, as out there, as something that could only happen in the dangerous jungles of Africa—what if MJ's journey was in fact parallel to our own? What if we approached engaging in our own context, with American whiteness, with being in relationship to our families, and dealing with the roots of this interconnected mess with the same purpose and courage that we will ascribe to MJ's life?
>
> And to take it one step further, what if we did so leaving the Martyrdom and Savior Complexes behind? What would that mean for those of us who are still in the land of the living?

Julia Kasdorf asks in her essay, "Mightier than the Sword: Martyrs Mirror in the New World" (2012),

> What if we claimed survival—even flourishing—as the fortunate inheritance of New World Mennonites? How would things change if, instead of asking our children, "What are you willing to die for?" we asked them, "What are you willing to live for?" or, "what new, beau-

tiful and just thing can you conceive here and now in this New World?"

What are these children for?

At three, Irene informed me that her daddy will die when all of his hair is white. Eventually he will, I agreed.

"But we won't die." She meant me, and herself, and Sallie, an eternal Trinity.

"We will," I told her gently. "Everyone will."

The terror in her eyes was real. "I don't want to die!"

I dropped the forks and spoons back into the dishwasher. I knelt down beside her as calmly as I could. "Everybody does," I told her. "You won't be alone," I promised recklessly. "I will be with you." Somehow, I will. I must find a way to meet her on some threshold between life and death.

She used to nap alone but began to insist I lie down beside her. She snuggled up and asked for the story of the Three Billy Goats Gruff day after day, until she had it memorized and began to tell it to me. The dialogue in her version was the same as in the folktale where the goat brothers defeat the troll: *"Who's that walking on my bridge?" "It is I, Little Billy Goat Gruff!"* —but when she told it, the troll ate all three of the goats who trip-trapped across her bridge. Then she, the troll, took a long, contented nap under the bridge. I hope Irene, my trickster, always rewrites the narratives, inserts herself into them in ways that work for her.

Sallie, oblivious to mortality at three years old, clomped sturdily into the world in her foot braces and perpetually runny nose. Her babysitter returned her to me one day, reporting that they were walking up the hill behind our campus when they encountered a visiting pastor and several of her friends returning from an intense prayer meeting at the top of the hill. The pastor felt a great burden. *There is so much world to change.*

Sallie broke away and ran to the pastor, reaching up her arms to be held. The pastor picked her up, and Sallie embraced her and would not let her go, held her until the pastor began to weep, until the other women said, "Here is Jesus in this child come to give you His love," and they took out a bottle of oil to anoint her for Christ's work. As they prayed over her, Sallie touched her fingers to their foreheads, as if she was anointing them in turn.

Three years old, and already commissioned.

And that's when I realized that the real question for me as a mother is not what our children are for but how to let go and let them do what it is already in their hearts to do.

Exhibit B: A note from MJ's mother Michele

Above all, my beloved son, I pray as you live and work amid all that is wrong in our world, that your daily journey brings you joy, joy as you serve!

Exhibit C: Sallie at Shalom, age two

I remember Sallie one day at church, two years old, after so long in physical therapy, finally on her feet walking—dancing, actually—in a ray of sun from the courtyard as we sang an Israeli folk song of gratitude: *Da-Dayeinu, Da-Dayeinu, Da-Dayeinu, Dayeinu, Dayeinu....*

The song got faster, and Sallie kept up, completely absorbed by the music. In that moment, my body couldn't possibly hold it all. The love was too big for the three bodies we had grown together. It was surrounded by the song of the people who made themselves ours with persistent casseroles, with careful words, with open arms—there was not enough space in my lungs for all the air in the room, and I knew that my face was leaking all over, but I really had to try to keep singing through the hiccups because I was a Mennonite.

I sang the body abundant, the body broken, this body. I sang for joy.

Joy, Sir Brother Pastor. That's the only thing we have any right to say that our children are for. The rest is up to them.

Our children are for joy.

23

Written On II

While I was not writing, life was writing on us.
My memory is non-linear at best.

At a training in 2022, Strategies for Trauma Resilience and Awareness (STAR), the facilitator Katie Mansfield asks us to imagine reaching out to take the hand of the oldest person we know, and then, with the other hand, to reach out to the youngest person we will ever know in the future. Seven generations, two hundred years, flash through my body, and suddenly I am trembling so hard that I have to leave the room.

* * *

The last time I saw Elaine, she laid quietly within herself in her hospice bed at home, eyes shut all day long. It was time to take the girls home, though Jason and Aunt Loretta would stay.

Christmas wasn't far off, but we had already had an early Christmas with her on Thanksgiving, put up her tree, and had her unwrap a framed photo of the twins that she particularly liked. She gave them coloring books. She was so fragile, it took a long time to tear off the paper, open the box, untangle the bubble wrap as the twins flitted back and forth between her and the coloring books. She loved Christmas. Later, when we moved Harold into the house beside ours, we filled an entire closet with her Christmas ornaments.

Before we said goodbye, we sang at her bedside, *Beautiful Star of Bethlehem*, in harmony, and from where she listened deep inside, she opened her mouth and tried to say goodbye, or say that she loved us, or ask for more music.

***

One morning, soon after, I told the girls that their grandma had died, and as we drove back to Louisa to join Jason and the family, I explained where she would be buried in the Powhatan Mennonite churchyard, with Grandpa beside her.

"But he's not dead!" Irene said in alarm.

I reassured her that we wouldn't bury him for a long time, not until he died, too, but they would rest beside each other in the end.

All was silent in the back of the car.

A few minutes later, she said, "Mom, can I be buried beside Sallie?"

There was snow when we arrived, and we built a snow cat with stick whiskers. Irene wondered why the hospital bed was still there, now that the body was gone. Sallie never asked for Elaine again, even when we visited the house.

Six years later, I'm still cooking with her canned tomato juice, baking with cornmeal from her freezer. She was most present, and most absent, in waves as I sorted provisions in her cellar when Harold moved—shelves of canned goods, two freezers, an extra fridge— taking some, throwing some away, the whole grains for grinding, frozen vegetables from her garden, sauces and soups and lots of creamed corn, and bags of tiny blueberries painstakingly picked.

***

When the cancer returned in 2016, this time in Elaine's bone marrow, the oncologist offered a new treatment, with optimism. "You'll be with us at this time next year," she promised.

Elaine bargained for more: "How about two years?"

The oncologist said, "I'm not going to play that game."

She made it a year, but not much more, not quite to the twins' fourth birthday. They were old enough to remember her a little, even outside of the photos and videos. A few years later, I asked Irene what she could remember of Grandma Elaine.

"Her kisses!" she replied immediately. "How she would hold me and kiss me and kiss me and kiss me."

***

Here's a literal snapshot: Grandpa Claude Beachy has come

to visit us in the valley. His children are taking him on a tour of assisted living communities, and here's a picture of him with my local Yoder grandparents, Morris and Janet, and their mutual great-grand-twins. Morris is propped precariously in his wheelchair, looking ready to slide right out of it, even as he grins his broad grin at Irene. Irene is about a year old, perched on Grammy Janet's lap, tiny pig-tails sticking straight up, holding a green ball and watching Sallie. Grandpa Claude has Sallie on his knee and is playing with her feet, their soles a blur for the camera, while she clings tightly to his forearms, her eyes wide, her mouth shut tight like a little trap.

Jason and I stand in the back, looking on. I'm looking in the same direction as Grandpa Morris, laughing at whatever made him laugh. Jason and Grammy Janet are the only ones paying attention to the camera. Jason's looking into the present, with an easy grin, but Grammy Janet is looking into the future, with a sense of occasion. She knows this will be a special picture, the only one the twins will ever have with their three living great-grandparents together.

When she looks at me today through the photo, straight in the eyes, I cry a few good tears, walk into my bedroom and place my hands on the frame of an old mirror from my great Aunt Helena, Morris's sister who lived for 99 years. The mirror frame might be the oldest thing we have in the house; the walnut comes from Peter and Lydia Nafziger's farm in Long Green, Maryland. The generations run from Lydia to Fanny Nafziger Hertzler, from Fannie to Irene Hertzler Yoder, to Great-Aunt Helena; when I touch the grain of this wood, I am holding two hundred years of our lives.

**

We made photo books for Irene and Sallie as each one of these elders passed into the great beyond, pages to help them remember the Great-Grandparents they were lucky enough to touch, beloveds born almost a century ago.

But the first photo book we made was for Grandma Elaine. As we composed the end of her book, we found the pattern of words we would end up placing at the end of every book: "We love Grandma Elaine, and we will always have her love."

24

Woman Built of Stones: A Mother Tries to Write

Mt. Pleasant, Pennsylvania

Four years after the twins' birth, two years before the pandemic, I'm supposed to be writing, but instead I stack stones under the banks of Jacob's Creek. In the shade of the laurels, I heft a rock onto a boulder base, then find the place where it will cup the curves of the next rock. It's hardest to stack them on their skinny edges to show their height and roundness, but possible. Each one has a balancing point, if turned tenderly enough to find it. I top the columns with spires of pebbles.

The simplest stack is four knobby rocks on a boulder, the topmost an oval like a face. To me, it's a woman, awkwardly poised, leaning uphill, caught in a moment where she can't balance for long.

On this weekend retreat, my first time alone since the babies came, I sleep twelve and thirteen hours each day. Even so, I'll write more material than I have in years. I'll share book recommendations, talk with mentors, take communion. But mostly, I'll remember stacking rocks alone in the cool streambed.

* * *

After supper, I text pictures of the rock towers to my twins and then call them. Irene chatters about their supper, then hands the phone to Sallie. *Mama,* Sallie says urgently, *Lala! Lala!* Aunt Loretta has come to stay. It's the first time she has ever tried to tell me a story about her day.

Sallie's genes are stacked up on the tricky edge. I still marvel that a human body can survive with an entire extra chromosome in the code; it should all tumble down. Yet she is healthy and growing, and today she tells me her first tiny story. Most of her limited language centers on food. At age two, she whispered dreamily in the middle of our morning snuggle, *Applesauce!* her first and last three-syllable word for another two years.

In the quiet of my private room, I review the study behind a clickbait headline about the Down syndrome "super genome." Most of us, for any given gene, have genetic expression that deviates as widely as 30-70 percent. Sallie's gene expression, however, runs tightly around the optimal 50 percent. Her entire genetic tower is centered enough to balance the weight of an extra stone on top. She is already a survivor.

Her body is soft and squeezable, and she smiles easily, but she isn't easy. Sometimes she refuses, fights me. I have slapped my solid, protesting, fragile child. We gave up naps because I could no longer bear to restrain her, even though I knew she needed more sleep than her twin. I'd lie next to her, singing, with an arm and a leg snuggled across her to quiet her, get her almost to sleep, and then Irene would burst into the room saying, "Mama, I need you!" and I would shout with frustration.

I was cruel every day, to both of them, and so I gave up on naps. Now, I think in the retreat center, I am only cruel on a weekly basis. Maybe if I could find time each day to go back to the river behind my own house and stack stones by myself, I would be cruel only once a month, once a year.

By morning, wind or wanderers will topple my rock spires into the creek, and I will start again.

***

That retreat, Poetics of Place at Laurelville, gave me hope that I would write again, even as a mother. I did, a little. A conference piece, turned sermon, turned essay, turned meditation, still not submitted. A revised piece about infertility, pending publication in a pandemic-delayed anthology. A passionate oped about school shootings crafted and sent in one hour, unpublished. A couple book reviews, here and there. A published poem. Attempted writing groups. A story honored in one competition, published much later.

The narrator of Rachel Yoder's *Nightbitch*, bereft of her artistic outlets by motherhood confesses, "I am angry all the time." Somewhere in those years, I scrawled on an envelope, "I am left feeling powerless a lot with my only recourse to bottle it up, take it out on someone smaller, or be bitchy or whiny—things unacceptable in women."

At a reading years ago, Sofia Samatar said that she wakes at 4:30 in the morning to write, so she need not resent her family or her students for keeping her from her work. Maybe it wasn't so early. Maybe she doesn't do that anymore. Maybe she falls asleep on the pages. But I cherish the image of a writer stealing, no, claiming her own time before anyone else.

During a short-lived experiment with morning pages when the girls went to kindergarten, I wrote about my own creative apathy:

> I'd rather at the end of the day plug into some sort of media than engage with creative activity or, you know, something resembling a life's work. I'd rather read a fourth article about Trump's tweet about Marie Yanakovitch than . . . revise that essay that I know is pretty darn good but that I've been holding off on.

And I reflected on balance, remembering a writing conference panel years ago where one mother said that writing was like going down into a deep well, leaving her children's demands up on the surface. I mustered my courage to ask the panelists how they balanced teaching, writing, and motherhood. One said simply, "I can't." She quit teaching.

Sometimes Jason would watch the twins, and I would trudge through our woods to sit by Briery Branch. It's our own creek, part of the Shenandoah watershed. Its bed is littered with river rock and, in places, patches of sand.

In the '80s and again in the '90s, Briery Branch overflowed its banks in catastrophic floods classified as 500-year incidents.

It's held in check by flood control dams built in the mountains above us. The insurance companies won't sell flood insurance to our neighbors who live directly under the dams, but they sell it to us.

Sometimes I stacked the rocks. Sometimes I scratched patterns in the sand with sticks. I tried to breathe. I brought a few flat pebbles home for the window ledge above the kitchen sink.

I thought things were getting better. And then it all toppled over.

***

In a Zoom session, faces are stacked in a grid with the bottom row smaller, but centered. For the first years of the pandemic, we stayed home and lived in Zoom. Jason and I took shifts working in our guest room office and supervising the twins' Zoom school. With Sallie, I Zoomed therapies and enrichment sessions. Around teaching, putting the finishing touches on 10-year reaccreditation materials and our institutional quality enhancement plan, and leading my university's general education revision, I helped Sallie complete each assignment, one painstakingly sounded-out word at a time. We told Irene she could skip school for the year if she wanted, but she wanted to keep her school iPad, where she illustrated little stories and created long journal entries.

People I loved died.

And Jason's father Harold had his first stroke. We spent our weekends packing his things and renovating a damaged house next door to us so that he could move in. A septic system replacement turned our side yard and field into a pile of rocks from our cobbly soil. The towers I built there were huge and heavy, and I was afraid they would smash the children's toes if they fell awry, so I stopped.

Instead, we danced. Each morning, I opened my laptop, and the girls and I added our faces and bodies to a grid of dancers from around the world. My colleague Katie Mansfield, who started this community, specializes in embodied strategies for building resilience. Years in, we still dance with Katie almost every day. We often end with the song, "Resilient," by Rising Appalachia, a meditation on staying centered in action. The song ends with a glorious roar, and the girls always come running to join us, jostling for position to show their teeth and claws to the camera.

The tagline for our group is borrowed from Alice Walker: "Hard Times Require Furious Dancing." In an essay (2013) with the same title, she writes about finding optimism in the face of suffering, loss, environmental devastation and challenging times "beyond the most creative imagination." In the essay, she considers the importance of dance to her community, and says of her own dawning awareness of it, "It isn't that I didn't know how to dance before . . . I just didn't know before how basic it is for maintaining balance."

Each pandemic morning, we shook the weariness or rage or frustration or anxiety out of our bodies. Balance, shift, find a new balance, keep moving.

When the twins remember the pandemic, they will remember that we danced every day. And they will remember their mother doing push-ups. After Justice Ginsburg died, I added push-ups to the dance. I grew up associating exercise with body hatred, so it seemed healthier not to exercise. But now I needed to live a long time, for the girls, for the fights to come. I stacked up the push-ups, a few more each week. Now I do forty on a good day.

Maybe it was the dancing, maybe it was strong biceps. Maybe the girls were growing up. I felt a little less out of control. Despite the chaos. Despite my mornings and evenings doomscrolling through the newsfeed. Each day, I balanced the necessary things, and let the rest lay scattered all around. Writing seemed unnecessary in the face of everything else.

* * *

One day I doom-scrolled my way past an article explaining why I shouldn't stack rocks:
- It promotes erosion.
- It intrudes on others' experiences of the natural landscape.
- You may be destroying food sources, hiding places, or nesting sites.
- In the eastern states, you might push the endangered Hellbender, a two-foot long salamander, into further decline.

- It may be culturally insensitive as cairns have been used for burial, navigational, and informational purposes by indigenous groups.
- Hikers may mistake your rock pile for a navigational cairn, lose their way, get caught in the wilderness after dark, and fall off a cliff, so...
- people might die.

I stopped stacking rocks.

* * *

After the attack on the Capitol, weary of news analysis, I started playing Candy Crush, a game that came pre-installed on my phone. In a grid of colorful candies, I matched three, and poof, they disappeared and new candies toppled down from the top. I collected cherries, smashed chocolate, and deployed the candy frog.

Studies show that you can reduce intrusive memories by playing Tetris in the hours following a traumatic event, like a car wreck or military engagement. The game activates a ludic loop—a short cycle with uncertainty and visual rewards that compels you to keep going. I felt the ludic loop at work when I played Candy Crush. A level took two to five minutes. It emptied the top layer of my brain, made everything hold still.

Within a year, I was 3000 levels in, at least 250 hours of play. You could spend 250 hours on monthly intensive writing retreats, or a year's worth of daily morning pages.

You could write so many letters to your representatives.

* * *

To open a meeting at work, I wrote a meditation on Matthew 26: "The eye is the light for the body." I talked about Candy Crush addiction and a day we lost Sallie's glasses. I ended it, tritely reverent, with "Christ be our light."

"You should publish that," said my colleague.

He said it, perhaps, because I referenced my daughter's disability. People like *real* sharing about disability, particularly if you can make it inspirational without making it inspiration porn,[10] Make it about hard work and hope without objectifying—much, or too obviously—the person with the disability.

Sallie's disability adds weight to any argument. I addressed our school board last fall, defending mask mandates and rights for trans kids from the perspective of access and inclusion. Out of a line of thirty speakers, the local news featured two clips: a rabble-rousing freedom lovin' anti-mask mama—and me, the well-spoken white mother of a child with a poster disability. Two Karens at their peak, in counterpoint.

I was proud. I felt dirty.

* * *

Maybe I resist writing because the things I want to write about now are someone else's story—a story that I want Sallie to be able to tell on her own someday.

* * *

I wrote those lines, then burst into tears. Was this the crucial discovery? The boulder at the base of the essay?

* * *

Then I highlighted them and typed, "Is this true???" It was an awfully convenient excuse to play Candy Crush and create nothing.

* * *

Our family of four walks back to Briery Branch on an unseasonably warm April afternoon in the upper 80s, the stream wide as a river with snowmelt today. The girls wear swimsuits, and Sallie tries out new water shoes.

For the first time, she wades independently onto the slippery rocks at the edge of the stream while Irene, out in the middle, shrieks at the icy current splashing up to her knees. Then Sallie takes my hand and leads me downstream toward the white water.

Later, I sit on the bank as Sallie pushes through the willows and invasive roses toward a rocky point she likes to explore. "Wait," Jason, calls, grabbing his brush axe. "I'll make you a path!" But Sallie is already forging ahead. Irene roars a mighty roar and leaps between rocks, grinning fiercely as she bruises her shins, undefeated.

I am writing this scene in my head as I witness it, although I won't scribble it down on paper for another day. I have signed up for a week-long writing faculty retreat in May, hoping to transform eight years of not-writing into an essay.

I take one stone and fit it to another, the tricky way, on edge. Then a smaller fat one on top, and a series of pebbles arcing up until it teeters and falls.

I decide that it is okay to stack stones here today. My little pile is nothing to what the next rainstorm will do. When the river is at its mightiest, you can hear the boulders rolling and grinding, and when the water subsides, new sand lines the banks, and all the rocks are stacked on edge leaning downstream.

We're not in hellbender territory, after all. My small creative efforts may disturb a crayfish or two but a) they can move and b) the fury of the next storm will transform their habitat so severely that they must adapt or die.

I want to raise adaptable children. We may not live directly under the dam of climate change and political unrest, but we live close enough to it.

I do care about Sallie's performance and behavior back in in-person school—it's part of what has been waking me, heart racing, at 5:30 in the morning—but what I really want to know is will democracy, such as it is, hold for her lifetime? Will the services available to her now—for all their inadequacies, so much better than they used to be—remain? Can I expect, with good life insurance, decent savings, and a long, healthy life of my own, to get her comfortably to the end of her days on the planet?

What about everyone else's Sallies?

If it all falls apart, will her vulnerability move my neighbors with their rebel flags and weapons stockpiles to be kind to her and, by extension, us?

What about all that she could have, if we keep building on our precarious progress? Self-driving cars to grant her independence? The Alzheimer's therapies, successful now in mouse models, that improve working memory?

Her future is balanced between potential and dread. How do I prepare her for it?

I sign her up for summer dance lessons.

25

Salt

Briery Branch, Virginia

This fall, on warm days, I often slip on a pair of my grandmother's sturdy rubber sandals when I start across the field to take Harold his supper. He's lived next door to us since that terrible pandemic year, when we moved him up from his home in Louisa. I have a pair of Elaine's sandals, too. I'm literally walking in dead women's shoes these days. They have borne the labor of care, and now they are beyond. They've become stories, and they walk with me in my own work.

Across the field where the bluebirds, pausing in their migration, perch on the poles of the fence where we used to keep the cow, then flutter up into the surviving walnut tree, Harold sits in his chair most of the day watching television. He once looked forward to mowing the lawns—his and ours—but he gave up the keys for now after a series of small strokes left him with extreme vertigo for a few weeks. The neurologist wants his blood pressure up to feed his brain; the cardiac clinic wants to keep it down to rest his heart. He just wants to get up and walk to the kitchen island to eat his dinner, but it's been hard lately.

Scoot to the front of your chair, I tell him, remembering another old man, another time not so long ago. Lean forward over your walker, nose over toes. Steady steps.

He's supposed to have a low-sodium diet, so perhaps it's for the best that he isn't driving these days to his favorite destinations, Arby's and McDonald's. Before he gave up the keys, I tried to tutor him, taking a harm reduction approach: a small burger and small fries has half the sodium of a Big Mac. The chicken sandwiches aren't safer. Sure, a gyro has vegetables in it, but it also has more salt than you're supposed to eat in an entire day. I buy his groceries as requested, but I agonize over the Lebanon bologna. In the end, I get the smaller pack. I advise him to eat no more than one slice a day. Not every day. His well-meaning neighbors send him salty soups, gravies, slices of country ham, chicken barbeque. I portion it out into small amounts, put most of it in the freezer.

* * *

A few months before her death, my grandmother, known as Grammy Janet to the girls, gave me her salt box. It's a white lidded ceramic pot, between cup- and pint-sized, with a black and white calf sitting on top to serve as the knob. Years ago, it held a novelty cheese, which she gave to her own mother Sallie, and she eventually inherited the box. She passed it down to me, still half-filled with her own salt, and with a label taped inside the chipped rim: *SALT,* hand-printed in thick, dark capitals.

We laughed, her blue eyes sparkling at me from beneath the deep veils of her eyelids. The label was new. The salt box was unlabeled back in my college days, when she lived just off campus and I would drop by frequently for a visit or snack, or to do my laundry. One afternoon she invited me to help myself to the berry cobbler cooling on her counter. I scooped a healthy portion into a cereal bowl, opened what I thought was the sugar bowl and sprinkled on a large spoonful, poured milk over the whole thing and took a hearty bite.

It was, of course, too salty to eat. She did, of course, offer me another healthy portion, unsalted.

* * *

Jason's mom, Elaine, was credentialed and practiced in nutrition, and with a family history of blood pressure issues, they kept "healthy salt" on their table, a formulation with half the sodium to sprinkle on her hearty, balanced meals. Harold ate well and healthily while she lived, although the wrappers on the floor of his truck were evidence that he ate well away from home, too.

Grammy Janet never had blood pressure issues, and I hope I inherited her constitution. So far it seems likely; my blood pressure is always low at check-ups, and sometimes if I stand up too quickly, I see stars. She was a thoughtful cook and never oversalted the food made for her guests, but she always added salt to her own portion at the table.

* * *

One day, when I'm making his grocery list —cereal, fruit juice, whole wheat bread, bagged salad—Harold asks, "Can you buy me some hot dogs?" I finally say no, that if he wants something hot instead of salads for lunch, I'll get him some low-sodium freezer dinners. But I question myself. Should we just let the man have what he wants? Eating is one of the remaining pleasures in his life.

* * *

In the cow shed, in the field between our houses, I find the mineral brick for the old cow still resting in the corner of the box where we'd scatter a few cups of grain for her on winter evenings. Hollowed by her tongue, but still hefty in my hand, its corner is furred with salt crystals almost two years past the last time she huffed her sweet-smelling bovine breath on it.

We had a cow for eight years, a little retired Dexter, a loner who didn't get along with her herd and just needed a meadow to mow. She hasn't come into my stories because she arrived when I was pregnant with twins; she was with us after the *before* and before this *after* (or it is *during?)*, when I can tell stories again. A carrier of chronodysplasia, her breeding had been mismanaged, and shortly after her arrival she gave birth to a stillborn calf with the genetic deformity—all cartilage, no bones.

She lived, mostly alone, in our back field. When the girls were older, they'd brush her furry winter hair in spring when it came out in clumps, and she'd close her liquid eyes in pleasure, and they'd feed her cornstalks from the garden and stroke her velvety nose and fuzzy ears, and she'd carry her horns so carefully around them, stepping delicately with all of her 700 pounds, since even a very small cow is big, compared to young humans.

According to her pedigree documents, she was just few weeks away from eighteen when she fell down in the snow and wasn't able to get up again. The vet who came out the next day wasn't able to give a clear prognosis—he'd never treated a cow so old. After a day or two, it was clear that she wasn't going to be able to get back up, and we called him to come back out and help her on her way. A neighbor with a backhoe dug a hole for us. Irene still lays cornstalks on her grave.

* * *

On All Hallow's Eve, we get a 5 a.m. phone call that Harold has fallen, courtesy of the company that responds to his call bell. They call the rescue squad, too. This time, it isn't vertigo, just a misstep. No injuries—he's not very breakable. Together, Jason and I hoist him up, warm up his oatmeal, and I go back to get the girls ready for school while Jason waits to tell the rescue squad never mind. It's just an early start to another day in our full life. I get the girls up to dance and eat breakfast, do my push-ups in between checking and stocking their backpacks. Sallie dresses as Bluey's mom, Chili, for school, but Irene saves her matching costume for trick-or-treating; she'd rather be a cat for school. Sallie still needs help with her shoes and toothbrush, and this morning we need to leave early so I can drive Jason to work after he drops off his car for inspection. In my blessedly quiet office at work, I brew a cup of tea. In theory, I have release time and this is to be a writing day, but instead there's a student recommendation to write and a meeting that must be scheduled. Not much later, there's another meeting about finding faculty to teach our dream gen ed course on systems and power; they're all so good, and stretched so thin. I join colleagues for lunch, talk of Halloween subdued by the recent death of a student in a car accident. There's time for a bit of editing before errands—picking up fruit at the store for dinner with friends tonight, checking out the new bookstore downtown and buying a couple lovely books with some of my research funding—and then it's time to pick up the girls, commute home long enough to organize Harold's supper, warm up a Healthy Choice—the lowest sodium I can find—crack open the lids of his fruit and salad for tomorrow's lunch, noting that he did eat a salad, fruit, and a boiled egg today. Back at the house, we empty the dishwasher, and while the girls practice piano or dance and have their screen time, I fill out the twenty-page Vineland 3 parent survey in preparation for tomorrow's meeting with the psychologist for Sallie's three-year eligibility review at school. It's too late to pick up Jason before the mechanic closes, so I swing by to pick up his key, pay for the car inspection and new tires—no time these days for Jason to order them himself. On the way back into town, the girls, now both dressed as *Bluey* characters, stop to trick or treat at my parent's house and then at my aunt's. We pick up Jason and visit our friends for Halloween dinner. It feels short, not enough time to catch up for a year's worth of changes. Sallie hates their cat, afraid it will rub its fur on her, I think. Irene can't leave it alone, sitting in the hallway beside it and petting and talking to it. When we go trick or treating in the neighborhood, it escapes the house and tries to follow us. We come here most Halloweens, but this is the busiest year we've seen, with so many houses in the neighborhood opening their doors, so many kids on the street even though it's chilly. A few blocks and two full baskets later, my ears are freezing and Sallie is exhausted. We say goodnight to our friends and add a loop to our commute home to pick up Jason's car. He stops at Harold's house to check his blood pressure and balance it out with his evening medicines according to a system he invented, and that the cardiac clinic endorsed after he ran it past them. While he gets Harold settled in bed for the night, I tuck the girls into their bunks late, with abbreviated stories and songs and, for once, follow shortly after instead of staying up too late on the Internet, one more day down in the books.

* * *

Our church, wonderful Shalom, asks if they can send us meals to help with Harold. Nope, I say, but I won't be bringing meals to anyone this year. And if I get sick, we're going to need lots of help. I go to a new integrative health nurse and take every supplement she recommends.

* * *

Irene likes me to sing *Ubi caritas,* a simple, repeated Taize song, for her bedtime most evenings, and I found myself singing it to the cow on the night that she fell. It had been a snowy, icy week, and she slid in the slush. The cold was breaking, turning toward a warm rain. I sat up into that night with the cow, in the cold that was getting warmer, in the rain, leaning against the weight of her living leather in my coveralls, trying to prop her up while Jason was doing something useful, now forgotten, and I sang to her, *Ubi caritas et amor, ubi caritas, Deus ibi est.*

(As I settle in to type about that night, try to feel the sense of it alongside the other losses of the pandemic years, sitting at our picnic table on the edge of the woods where the wind rustles the sycamore leaves, my phone rings. Harold is having trouble with his razor, and Dish Network isn't working and all he can get is a Christmas train screensaver, no Fox. By the time I return, my two hours to write has diminished to twenty minutes before the girls need lunch, and that golden melancholy meditative feeling has seeped away.)

The old loner cow was down and seemed ready to go that night, but I kept vigil with her, tears for once coming easily with the rain. Eventually we rigged up a shelter, and the next day managed to move her into her cow shed by rolling her into the front-end loader of the tractor and carrying her, cradled like a baby, across the field, then tipping her carefully into the deep straw.

* * *

We sang to Grandpa Morris, too, at least once, maybe several times at the end of his life. We weren't sure if we were at a deathbed or not. His was a slow decline, with no extreme measures, just palliative care in the nursing home. I don't even remember the call, when it eventually came. I think of him when his fall crocuses bloom in our yard.

One old friend, who I hadn't spoken to for years, died alone in the cold during the pandemic. Long ago, he gave me a pair of hand-knitted mittens. The moths chewed holes in the wool, but I couldn't throw them away. I've mended them with salvaged yarn, visible blue patches. They are keeping my hands warm this fall. I think of him when spring crocuses bloom, as they did when I heard the news.

A childhood friend died during the pandemic of a heart condition. Her young daughter found her in the morning. I sent her daughter lilies of the valley for a fairy garden, all the way to the

West Coast. (As I type, my own child arrives, hangs around for five minutes, then announces loudly that she is hungry, *hangry*, and I must come to feed her. I am breathtakingly shamelessly grateful that I still get to be in her life.) I think of my friend every time I see a good classic Star Wars meme—and when the lilies of the valley bloom.

I don't know what order these losses happened in; my memory doesn't work that way, but the person that I remember most constantly, and with such strong presence that there's little room for sadness, is Grammy Janet, who joins me in the kitchen daily when I open the salt box, take her half-teaspoon scoop, and scatter the grains into the soup or the dough. I use less these days, for Harold, but you still need a little, to bring out the flavor.

* * *

Jason likes to tell a story about when we were dating: on one of our long drives, we stopped somewhere for a quick lunch, and he saw me eat French fries for the first time. I opened a packet of salt and shook it down through the box of fries, powdering them thoroughly. He laughed; he thought I was making a dramatic statement, over-salting with irony something that was already far too salty.

I was not. I like my fries so salty that they burn. I like the way that the salt in the packets at McDonald's comes in fine crystals, so they spread like powder. I like to lick the salt from my fingers, and then dredge my fingers in the salt-powdered bottom of the box and taste it again.

Now he understands how much I need to savor it. Sometimes he takes the mortar and pestle and grinds the salt from Grammy's box extra fine, for me to dip edamame in, feel it flare on my tongue.

* * *

Ever since she was a baby, Irene has had the ability to cry in fountains, to wet her hair and clothes, to make pools of gigantic, copious, salty tears. She's a big kid now and doesn't cry much, but her tears are still enormous. Somewhere between baby and big kid, Irene told me, "When I am sixteen, I will be able to drive. I will get into a car, and drive away. And I'm taking Sallie with me." When she was smaller, she told me that she'd marry Sallie when she grew up, and I laughed and told her she didn't have to—Sallie was already family. She could marry someone else, if she finds someone she wants to add to the family.

Just last year, Sallie and I had the same conversation when she confided that she would marry Irene when she grew up. Now, almost ten, Sallie tells me that she wants to live with her crush from school when she grows up, and she also says she will drive at sixteen. I don't correct her, because I don't know what will be true for her. She tells her speech therapist that salt is purple, and her therapist thinks she's wrong, but she's right—the specialty grape-infused salt in the grinder on our table *is* purple.

I don't know how Sallie's story will play out. I don't know if a time will come, in a few short years, when the only person I need to take care of every day is myself. Or maybe that time will never come. Maybe I'll look back on these as the easy years, when the girls were in school most days and I could hold down a job, cook dinner, and walk across the field most evenings. When, on the short walk back to our house, the work of the day would lift off into a sky that was spangled with stars or fading from blue to gold or maybe ranged with lavender streaks above the mountains.

* * *

We reached a milestone today: when I dropped off Harold's supper of baked fish, broccoli seasoned with Mrs. Dash's original salt-free seasoning, nine-grain bread, and cherry tomatoes, he showed me what his neighbor had dropped off: a quart of salty bean soup and a pack of country ham slices. "Take them away," he said. "Give it to Jason. See what he says."

I asked if he wanted a little taste of the ham.

"Already had one," he said. "That's enough." He did the exercises the physical therapist left for him. He's making an effort. Despite the difficulties, he wants to stay here, where, on a sunny day when he's feeling well, he can get out and ride around on his John Deere Gator, visit his neighbors. He hopes to mow the lawn again this summer, now that we've beat the vertigo. I tell him we'll bake a cake when he reaches 100 days with no falls. He's getting close.

* * *

After my grandpa moved into nursing care, Grammy Janet lived alone, half-widowed. The first time I visited her in her new solitude, I found her baking. Mincemeat pies, she explained, because Morris never liked mincemeat. If she was going to live on her own, she'd find the advantages. She's peering out at me now from the wall, her eyes twinkling between laugh lines, my mother's and the twins' and my own face squeezed together with hers in the frame of a selfie. She was always curious and, I think, always a bit amused. She'd watch where the sun rose behind Massanutten mountain throughout the year, track the movement of its path or the depth of the snowfall, take notes on the phases of the moon. She recited witty poetry and only ever said good things about other people.

Her salt box never empties. Whenever it gets a little low, I refill it and stir it thoroughly, guaranteeing that I will forever use a bit of Grammy's salt to cook our meals. I will send some of this salt with my daughters when they leave home, along with starts from her aloe vera, and Elaine's sansevieria, and Grandma Edna's Christmas cactus, and Grandpa Morris's fall crocuses, and the snowdrops—well, maybe just the salt, for starters, after all. And if I'm blessed to live into my nineties, as Grammy did, and the time comes to give up my possessions, I'll put a little of that salt into a shaker and keep it in my cardigan pocket with my reading glasses and whatever passes for a phone in the 2070s. Even if they tell me I need to stop using salt, I'll add a little, just a little, just enough to bring out the flavor.

26

Simple

Here they are, bursting through the school doors, twinned energy sprinting across the carline crosswalk to where we wait to pick up the big kids. As usual, Irene is flushed with excitement from beating her jump-rope record, or playing recorders in Music, or a Mars habitat she designed in Challenge, or a scheme she's made with this year's best friend; Sallie shouts goodbyes and pretends to steal noses from everyone—the crossing guard, the principal, the teachers on their walkie-talkies. The principal tries to protect his nose, but it's too late—she's carrying it triumphantly in her upraised fist.

Today, everyone is pointing at the clouds, strange white strands twisting below a high grey sky. I won't be able to identify them, even consulting in our field manual of clouds at home.

"Mom!" Sallie shouts, plastering herself against my window. "Mom, mom, mom, mom, mom! January 12. New Blueys!"

"Yes! Wonderful! Get in the car. Buckle your seatbelt. People are waiting." This year, finally, finally, Sallie can buckle her own seatbelt, given enough time. It's a good thing I usually end up near the end of the car line, cutting it close from some meeting or project at work, so too many people don't have to wait for us. Today she doesn't fumble for long before the belt is snapped in place and we're off. It's Friday afternoon, ten new episodes of Bluey have dropped, and the clouds are epic.

Irene snaps shots of clouds on my phone as we drive—this one like a dragon, this one like an enormous eye. She's learned to see the sky above the valley like I do—clouds that look like mountains, mountains that look like clouds. Last week, she was the first to point out a golden mountain in the sky.

At home, I butter the popcorn, and all three of us pile on the couch to watch the new adventures of this cartoon family of Blue Heelers from Australia. The girls are wearing Bluey ears from trick-or-treating in October. Sallie's are orange for Chili, the mother of the family—the practical one whose patience sometimes stretches thin at the antics of her daughters and her easygoing partner, Bandit. Irene is blue-eared Bluey, the big sister. My personal favorite is Bingo, a youngest sister like me, large eyed, alternately bursting with glee and struggling to keep up.

In one of the new episodes, "Relax," Chili can't seem to shake off her responsibilities after the family arrives at their beach condo. Alone on the beach, her body rigid with tension, she tries to read a book entitled *How to be Happy*. The theme music for this episode is based on the Shaker tune, "Simple Gifts," with jaunty motifs accompanying the children as they race from room to room discovering bunk beds, tiny soaps, and bath bubbles; then culminating in the full flowing melody when Chili, after a struggle, finally seems ready to go with the flow, settling onto a lounge chair on the balcony with a hot drink. The closed captioning says, "motivational music plays." "Simple Gifts" returns in the credits in a final variation as "whimsical music."

Simple as a song

It's one of the theme songs of my life. We sang it often from the green *Sing and Rejoice* book when I was growing up in Paoli. *'Tis a gift to be simple, 'tis a gift to be free, 'tis a gift to come down where we ought to be* is a good song for Granola Mennonites, even if they sometimes try to sneak some harmony into the single line of melody printed in the book.

Our high school marching band played a thematically similar song, "Simple Song" from Leonard Bernstein's Mass, as a quiet interlude in our Bernstein-themed show during my first of many seasons playing the bells, xylophones, and cymbals in the front-line ensemble. Before we competed at state finals, my mentor from church gave me a note with the full lyrics in it, words about improvising a simple song for God.

I still have my mentor's card somewhere, in one of several cardboard boxes of mementos that my parents, streamlining their lives for retirement to the Valley (*of love and delight*), transferred from their basement to my cramped storage space under the eaves. It would be a daunting task to find it—the boxes of memories and souvenirs and books are packed four high and three deep in a long row, in a space where you have to hunch down to avoid the slope of the roof, the crawl-space freezing in winter and boiling in summer. I'd like to sort through the collection and streamline my life like my parents have. The storage space under the eaves of their new house is carpeted and insulated, and the few items kept there—suitcases, Christmas decorations—have spaces in between them.

I think about cleaning mine out, but those old craft supplies from Grammy Janet might come in handy sometime, and no one else wanted to keep that comforter made for Grandpa when he was a boy, and we already gave away so many of the vases from Elaine's flower-collecting days that we have to keep the rest, and I don't throw away handwritten letters and Jason doesn't throw away Christmas cards, and those obsolete textbooks represent all the knowledge I could have acquired in college.

Besides, there's not actually any time to sort it out.

Simple as a strand of white lights

Simplicity was a virtue: simplicity in house, in dress, in food, in decor, in budgeting. We strung our Christmas cedar with white lights and delicate ornaments in reds, whites, greens, and gold. Some homes in the neighborhood were decked out with blinking colored lights, aluminum candy canes, life-sized plastic pastel manger scenes, roof Santas and snowmen, with Rudolph and the gang prancing across the lawn, and more glitter added every year to the aging collection. My sister and I said unkind things about these homes while we waited for the bus, taking cues from our parents' aesthetic.

We rolled our eyes at this unnecessary display, just as I scorned the extravagance of powder, blush, eyeliner, mascara, of bangs curled, teased, and hairspray-cemented, dramatic '80s fashions arriving in Southern Indiana in the early '90s. I didn't know how to do it, so it felt convenient to disdain it. My sister learned to navigate fashion, low-key and on the cheap. She chose a few good things, taking the best of the current trends. I diverged into a competing kind of simplicity, making my own styles from vintage finds, rag-picking, ransacking my mom's college clothes, sometimes borrowing from the drama club costume collection.

Jason was acquainted with my sister in college before I arrived in the valley. Based on a sample size of one, he believed that Paoli, Indiana, must be a place of wealth and understated stylishness. People from Paoli, he could see, were well put together. And then I walked into the dining hall a couple years later, likely wearing an oversized button-up shirt, Indian print skirt, long hair trailing, battered sandals, probably a scarf or two, and he was incredulous. That couldn't be Liz Beachy's sister. From Paoli?

Years later, when inflatable lawn ornaments came into vogue, I called my sister from my grad-school rental in Morgantown, West Virginia, and gave her a play-by-play as my neighbor set up his decorations one Thanksgiving weekend. Peering out the window, in tones of horrified fascination, I described each bulbous beast that he deployed in the empty lot beside his house. These new-fangled atrocities were worse than our old neighbors' displays. During the day, my neighbor turned off the power and the decorations lay flaccid, face-down on the lawn. Each night they arose turgid, glowing, undulating gently in any breeze. I've seen so many since then, it's hard to remember the specifics, but I believe there were Santas and reindeer and bears bearing gifts. I don't recall any sacred imagery in the inflatables. Who would want to deflate baby Jesus, after all?

Simple as a smart girl curling her bangs

In fifth grade, in the lunch line, a girl told me that I could easily get boys to like me if I would just curl my bangs and stop talking about how smart I was. Seven observations:
1. I must have liked talking about how smart I was. It may have been my primary way of interacting with boys. I probably wanted to compare math scores. Because we

didn't have a television, my main model for romance was Anne Shirley, who always tried to beat Gilbert Blythe in the spelling bee. To win a guy's affections, you had to dominate him intellectually, then crack your slate over his head.
2. I don't remember talking to boys, at all, after this.
3. I did come in third in the tri-state regional spelling bee a few years later, just one place away from nationals.
4. I never could curl my bangs, not properly, even with a load of hairspray. I had this recalcitrant cowlick that swept half of my bangs away from my forehead.
5. Ironically, the one boy who invited me to "go with" him in fifth grade decided I was smarter than his current girlfriend of the week and requested an upgrade. I declined. He was cute, but I was pretty sure our people didn't "go with" anyone.
6. Someone got to that girl in the lunch line, maybe the same person who made sure her socks always matched her scrunchie; someone had convinced her that her smarts made her less desirable—and she had smarts. She was one of the "gifted and talented" kids and later would compete with our team at science fairs and academic bowls. But she kept her intelligence on the down-low.
7. 'Tis a gift to be simple, but is it simple to be gifted?

Simple as life without television

In fifth grade, I was a newcomer to the insular community of Paoli (population 3000, high school gymnasium capacity 5000, because basketball). That boy who liked me for a week couldn't believe I didn't have a television. I'd already had to explain to him that Mennonites didn't use buggies like the Amish who made their small farms among the rolling hills of our county. I told him what my parents told me—when they got married, they were too poor to buy a television. I didn't tell him the rest, that Dad's parents were missionaries in Haiti, that Mom's family had lost their dairy farm in a bad land deal, that they never saw the need to buy a television later—too much background noise for my mother, who needed quiet to focus. Better for their children to grow up in a world of books. We claimed it as a mark of distinction: growing up without a TV made us smart.

The boy called me "Too Poor to Buy a TV" after that, which was funny to all of us. My uncle was a well-known doctor in this economically depressed community, so folks assumed Beachys had plenty of money. What I didn't understand was that we actually did. Sure, cash flow was tight because we were paying off a custom-built house on one parent's salary while the other one stayed home. But we had nutritious food from the garden, church camp in summer, good healthcare, and could always tithe and more. I didn't understand when one of my friends told me my life made her feel like a kid looking in a candy store window. She had a TV in her bedroom and we could watch as much MTV as we wanted until we got bored and did another dramatic read-through of *Rosencrantz and Guildenstern are Dead*.

Yes, that play made it into my backwater of southern Indiana, recommended by one of the smart kids I met at science fairs. We meet each other at competitions and music camps and exchange letters. This was before the Internet, mostly, but Dad was an early adopter, and sometimes I'd go on the dial-up and print out emails from them. At school, I made my home with the marching band, drama club, and every academic team. We studied calculus and "Mending Wall" and read Li-Young Lee. We traveled around the state, to Ontario, to California with my milk-preservation science research projects, meeting up again and again with the other smart kids. We were all going to college on scholarships, most of us planning to leave the state.

A newspaper clipping from the *Indianapolis Star* on the state's academic All-Stars featured our family and several others who raised multiple All-Stars. The common theme—no televisions. We took it for granted that TV rotted your brain.

Simple as a detour in the West Virginia mountains

I loved being smart. I loved tests, I loved gold stars, I loved creating science projects and writing clever columns for the Paolite student paper, eating candy with the academic superbowl team in the library, competing for scholarships. But I didn't go to college right away. I thought, eventually, I might be a microbiologist. But when my research advisor told me, in my senior year, that he was going to invest in an electrogel phoresis system for DNA analysis, and that this would be my year to use it, I declined. I opted to do another spoiled-milk project, keep things low-key, lose myself in books and music and theater. I had too much going on, wanted to simplify.

The next year, I went to Philippi, West Virginia, to do a year of service, helping out in an elementary school and at a food pantry. By the time I emerged from that particular house church of Appalachian Granola Mennonite mystics, I didn't care about DNA. I was a philosophy major and then added a theater major, then found out I'd always been a writer. And now, so much time has passed that I fear it's probably too late to go back to school, to do research on brains, to untangle the amyloid plaques that cause cognitive issues and early onset Alzheimer's disease in people with Down syndrome.

Simple as a Mennonite dream

A friend, a Granola Mennonite smart girl, my mentor's daughter, stayed in Paoli. She found another Granola Mennonite at Goshen Gollege, came home, sustainably built a house of straw, had twins a year before I did, and they support themselves through farming and art. They're living the dream.

Some of our friends here in the Valley farm vegetables for market, keep flocks of sheep, don't have to buy supplemental beans and tomatoes because their gardens aren't neglected. Their backyard flocks aren't expensive pets but productive collaborators in a permacultural harmony. We don't even have backyard livestock right now: our beehives are empty, and we finally hauled the crumbling chicken coop to the dump.

I realize I have a very clear picture of The Dream, actually, in the back of my head, now that I'm thinking about it. My mental Granola Mennonite Dream Scorecard looks something like this:

Granola Mennonite Dream Scorecard

See how well you are keeping up with the Umoja-Yoder-Schmatlzfuses!

BACKYARD LIVESTOCK

• Produce income or at least save money	+5
• Cost more than they save, but have a bucolic vibe	+2
• Don't have them; too much trouble	+0
• Killed by predators	-5

FOODWAYS

• Vegan	+5
• Only eat meat that you butchered	+5
• Most of your food comes from your home	+3
• Most of your food is grown locally	+2
• Bake your own goods (homemade carbs fine)	+2
• Most of your food is processed externally	-5
• Locally owned restaurant with locally sourced food	+5
• Locally owned restaurant	+2
• Fast food	-5

GIFTS

• Made it yourself	+5
• Bought at local stores	+2
• No-waste packaging	+3
• Wrapped with repurposed materials	+3
• Thrifted	+4
• Dumpstered	+5
• Amazon Prime	-5

TITHING

• No income to avoid paying war taxes	+5
• Voluntary gas tax	+3
• 10%	+3
• 25%	+5
• Public Radio and Planned Parenthood count as tithes	+2
• Remembering to give when you like the sermon	-2

DOMICILE

• Spacious, simple, uncluttered	+5
• Well-insulated and sustainably built	+5
• Solar panels	+5

- Rainwater retention system   +5
- Heated with renewable resources   +5
- Floor covered with Bluey toys, books, artwork   -5

EMPLOYMENT

- Sustainable community-based farming   +5
- Global development or sustainability work   +5
- Peacebuilding/Restorative Justice   +5
- Mennonite church institution   +3
- Anything else, except...   +0
- Military   -10

Let's tour the homes of these model Granola Mennonites: this one making cheeses, that one unschooling her children, another one sending their kids to forest school. She's organizing protests in D.C.; he's organizing protests downtown. They're raising goats, they have an orchard and a nursery, all have CSAs. They provide the community with organic blueberries, they drive electric vehicles. Lots of us are on the way to full electric: see all the hybrid Priuses lined up in the church parking lot? They're installing solar all over the East. He's working on housing for the local unhoused population, she's managing an interfaith peace camp. They're investing in shade-grown coffee. They're out of the country doing relief and development work.

What absolutely amazing people! Do any of them feel like they're doing enough? Are any of us free from this frantic sense that more must be done? Probably not. Because we know that we're living with wealth. Much has been given to us—family land, or good education, or good health, or relatively stable childhoods, or strong, supportive social networks, sometimes all of the above. Much is required. How much is enough?

"Good enough," my high school band director would say, "is neither." He's not Mennonite, but he gets it.

Simple as a freezer meal

My parents kept careful count of the grocery money when I was little. Things felt tight, but that tightness was part of the virtue. Live within your means so you have enough to give away—at least the biblical 10 percent tithe (+3), but ideally more, much more (+5). They have a comfortable retirement, but my mom is still so careful with the grocery money that when we go grocery shopping, I want to lecture her about inflation.

These days, I buy groceries heedless of the cost, and we eat out weekly (local restaurants, +2). My deep freeze is full of foods you can put on a tray and bake in 20-30 minutes (-5), not chickens we raised and butchered ourselves. Some of it is in an effort to support two professional lives, growing twins with ballet and piano lessons running into the evening hours, and the old farmer next door who doesn't cook for himself. Some of it is an attempt to buy back a little more time to enjoy life with the girls while they're young. We have more money than time, and yet we wonder if we have enough of either. Having a child that with lifelong needs changed our calculus, and instead of leaving my job to raise children and gardens, I decided to keep an outside career going as long as possible. We live in a small house with no debt, banking our dollars and hours against the unknown future instead of giving our surplus freely.

But sometimes, we pay for things that never would have been in the budget when I was growing up in Paoli: eating out, so many Internet streaming services, the beach every year, tickets to see Sallie's favorite, Laurie Berkner, in concert, a trip to Charleston, West Virginia, to see *Bluey's Big Play*.

Simple as play

Sallie researches all things Bluey online, and she was the one to show me clips of *Bluey's Big Play* on YouTube, to insist that we go see it. It tours around the country, hitting major population spots, none of them near us. She brought it up weekly, daily, hourly. She needed to see *Bluey's Big Play*. Then we found out that the last two days of the school year had been canceled, which meant that it would be remotely plausible for us to see the play on its tour date in Charleston, West Virginia, four hours away.

I reserved a hotel room and bought tickets, just three, because Jason was amid a job transition, leaving his Mennonite college job (+3) after 23 years and going to work at the big university across town (+0, but better for our savings account).

The long drive to Charleston was worth it. We took old Route 60 to picnic at the New River Gorge, took a short hike to see the bridge spanning the deep gorge and listen for train whistles echoing up from the river far below. We played in the children's museum, Irene ascending to the top of the atrium on the climbing sculpture, Sallie driving the firetruck and serving burgers in the diner, both of them producing a convoluted play on the children's stage about the secretly evil butterfly queen and the servant who defeated her.

The start of the grand event, *Bluey's Big Play*, was delayed a bit because of the time needed to seat the multitudes of parents and children who had made this pilgrimage with us. After three years of pandemic, it felt strange, but liberating, to be crowded so closely in an auditorium together. Sallie vibrated with joy for the entire 45 minutes of the play. I can prove it; I have video. The production is beautifully done, with human companions bringing life to people-sized puppets of the Heeler family and friends, color-saturated sets, soaring shadowplay flocks of birds, and a message about lifting up your siblings that adults and children can both take to heart—but my video clips don't capture most of it. Mostly, I'm filming the grin that Sallie flashes at the camera when she sees my phone, then turns back to the stage, watching intently, flapping her hands along with the theme music, gasping and clutching her shirt as the characters fight for control of the magic xylophone, pointing and shouting and grimacing, clamping her hands over her ears for the noisiest, favorite bits with Bluey's loud toy, Chattermax.

The next morning, she woke up and asked if we could go see it again. I had to tell her no, but at least we could ride the elevator downstairs and make waffles for breakfast. Almost as much as she loves Bluey, Sallie loves packing her suitcase and staying in hotels.

Irene likes hotels, too, but she makes me check for bedbugs. Irene inherited the traits that made me smart at school, and she also has a keen interest in how things fit together—Jason's systems and mechanical know-how. Somewhere, from neither of us, she picked up an interest in running. She ran the most laps in her grade in jogging club and has beads on a necklace to prove it, and she wears that necklace to school most days, almost a year later.

I never suggest she should hide her trophies. She earned third place among the six Geography Bee finalists at her school, ahead of the rest of the fourth graders. She chain-reads her book series and thinks up math problems while she waits to go to sleep. She can identify every bird that visits our suet feeder and has made up personal names for many of them. When her classmates wrote anonymous compliments for each other, she was irritated to find they were all the same, saying she was smart. Only one offered a little variety—it said she was kind, "But that was from my teacher," she complained. "I recognize her handwriting."

When we returned from West Virginia, their final report cards and standardized test scores were waiting in the mail. On the standardized tests, Sallie scored in the 0th percentile on the test she had started to take—before shutting her laptop and declining to continue. We waived her second test. Irene had high scores on everything, perfect scores in math.

We tell them to be kind, curious, and creative. We praise them when they work hard. We are so proud of both of them.

We started Irene on piano lessons later than most kids—first Covid got in the way, and then life. But she picked it right up last fall, blew through the primer and is well into the first level, relished her first two recitals, and takes her practice time seriously. She works hard. Sometimes she'll call me over to help her figure out a difficult passage. After one session where I tried to explain a challenging rhythm, she got so frustrated with my convoluted explanation that she called a halt, closed the piano, and left the room, saying with dignity, "I am going to go talk to a more simple human!"

Within moments, she and Sallie were taking the Bluey family on a roadtrip upstairs in their landrover, going to visit the big dollhouse. Soon, tiny bunk beds and toilets and lawn furniture, alongside the ubiquitous piles of picture books, had been arranged across the entire floor of their tiny bedroom (-5) and the two would play together until I called them away for lunch, return to their imaginary world in the afternoon, and only with prompting, clean up the mess in the evening at bedtime.

Simple as dancing when the music starts
I loved that Irene used the word simple for Sallie. I like the word *simple* for Sallie, and I like simple best as it applies to Sallie. I'm probably not supposed to use it, though. "Simpleton" still has a sting to it, but is so outdated it's rarely used, even in insults. The term doesn't even appear in disability style guides where other offensive or dated terms—"mentally retarded," "cretin," most uses of "handicapped"—are labeled as verboten.

Simple is on trend, after all—the early 2000s brought us a host of simple living magazines, then Marie Kondo with her *Life-Changing Magic of Tidying Up* told us to simplify our possessions to include only those that spark joy, and now we're all aspiring to uncluttered spaces and schedules and Inbox Zero.

Simple is true to how Sallie's brain works, as I understand it. I often have three different channels open at once: composing a text to my parents while waiting to hear whether Irene will decide on toast or cereal as I'm coaxing Sallie to drink her elderberry supplement, and I only get overwhelmed when Jason cuts in on a fourth channel to ask where he can find the leftover pasta to pack for his lunch.

But Sallie has only one channel available. If she's chewing goldfish crackers, we have to turn off the music. If I run the windshield wipers while she's listening to music in the car, she shouts at me. A persistently buzzing fly can ruin her picnic, and she'll put on a beanie cap on an eighty-degree day if the smallest breeze blows through her hair.

On Sallie's single available channel, she is all in. When dancing, she's dancing. When reading, she can't be pulled away from her book, and when she is watching *Bluey*, God forbid anyone take the tablet away from her. If she is protesting something, she will remain stolidly in her state of refusal as long as you argue or coax. It's only when you turn away that she'll be free to consider other options. And if she's offering love—a snuggle or a chat, perhaps—she will melt into your eyes and arms and stay forever.

After school, she has a routine: she puts her bag and shoes away, goes to the bathroom and washes her hands, puts away the silverware from the dishwasher, practices dance for ten minutes, and has her reward—twenty minutes of educational screentime. After that, she goes out to swing and sing and talk to her Barbie, sometimes for hours. She's gone through three Barbies now—they lose thumbs, hair, and ultimately their legs as time passes. She needs empty time and space by herself to process the day, imagine things, or play her favorite songs.

She has a glorious sense of humor. One morning, she showed up at breakfast wearing her panties on her head, and we all laughed. The second morning that she showed up with panties on her head, I had to explain that things are funniest the first time and less funny when repeated. She got the point and retired the bit. She calls me "Bad Mom," dramatically, when I forget her morning milk. She turns people into animals with her magic asparagus or freezes them into statues with her magic, both games learned from Bluey.

When she is hurt or upset, the grief pours out in torrents, and then, like a switch has flipped, she's over it. She wipes her eyes, says, "I'm okay," and she moves on.

School has been complicated at times; Sallie isn't. The main challenge is to organize everything else around Sallie's flow.

Sallie loves a good chicken tikka masala (local restaurant, +2) or getting burgers (fast food, -5). She believes in hugs, and makes it her business to invite every family member into the hug. Whenever we pack our suitcases, the excitement is palpable. She loves to camp, she loves the beach, she loves to see a show, she loves road trips—especially when she gets to pick the music. She counts down the days to the next big things: Season 3 of "Is it Cake?" at the end of March and her dance recital in May. She loves holidays and costumes and presents and celebrations. Every good thing is entirely good while Sallie is experiencing it.

As long as she lives with us, this is what I can expect from life, every day: music, dancing, deliciousness, snuggles, adventure. The calculation that shapes our life today is its own kind of simple. Keep the music playing, the books on the shelf, the food on the table, suitcases packed for adventure as long as we can.

I read somewhere long ago that the brain activity of subjects with Down syndrome was the same as Buddhist monks in the deepest levels of meditation. This is quite possibly apocryphal, because I haven't been able to find further details on this. And maybe brain scans are unreliable science anyway: last week, I heard on the radio about a study in which researchers used statistical noise in the data from an fMRI calibration procedure to demonstrate that the brain of a dead salmon could recognize and respond to photos of human emotions. The available studies on brain activity of subjects with Down syndrome are dense and difficult for me to interpret—remember, I opted out of the sciences after all—but they typically end with a discussion of these brains as "underdeveloped" or "underperforming."

All proper caveats aside, it would make a satisfying story, wouldn't it? That Sallie's neurodiverse brain, the one that makes math take so much longer, also allows her to have immediate access and closeness to the essential nature of reality, a peculiar focused openness and oneness that the greatest practitioners take years of training to achieve? Wouldn't it be nice to think that she is somehow, already, just by virtue of being herself, closer to the Divine than the rest of us?

The lyrics of Bernstein's "Simple Song" taught me that nothing is more simple than God.

Simple as a sentimental film

"Simple Song" was originally written for *Brother Sun, Sister Moon* before Bernstein left the project. The 1973 Zefferelli film about the life of St. Francis was praised by some for its simple beauty but panned by the authoritative Roger Ebert, who gave it only two stars, criticizing it as a "big, limp Valentine of a movie," too full of "sweetness and light." *The New York Times* reviewer Vincent Canby said the film was "the sort of movie that tries to make poverty look chic, and almost goes broke in the attempt" and "confuses simplicity with simplemindedness."

Before I left home for a year of service, the Paoli Mennonite church gave me a gift, the prayer of St. Francis, beautifully calligraphed and framed. *Make me a channel of your peace,* etc. hangs in my kitchen today, along with our Navajo sand painting of Father Sky, below the gargoyle that glowers down on our cooking space, warding off bad taste.

When true simplicity is gained
"Tis a Gift to be Simple" is a Shaker dance. In the earliest years, Shakers danced as the spirit led in movements that outsiders critiqued as wild and promiscuous; later, their dances were choreographed and rehearsed, with motions connected to the meaning of the songs—which outsiders then critiqued as uniform and monotonous. I watch a Shaker dance workshop online. The students dance in concentric circles, "sisters" moving in one direction in the center, "brothers" stepping in the opposite direction on the outside, their hands outstretched before them to receive their simple gifts. Then they face center, *bow and bend*, twirl one way, then the other, and land on the right foot so that by *turning, turning,* they *come round right*.

Our Dancing Resilience group recently had an in-person gathering. To celebrate four years of dancing together on Zoom with people from thirty different countries and about as many states, around twenty of us, mostly women from across the South and the Midwest, converged for an evening and a day of dancing, eating, talking, learning, juggling, singing, laughing, crying, napping, listening, and remembering.

When the pandemic started, Katie Mansfield and a few of her friends decided to dance on Zoom, five times a day, at first with the idea of choreographing something, soon simplifying that to just putting on a playlist and dancing to the shared music. The girls and I joined a few weeks in and have been dancing ever since, although by now we just dance in the mornings.

Often the girls are eating breakfast while the dance is on, and I intermingle stretching, push-ups, and dancing with buttering toast and brushing hair. When the right song comes on, one or both of them will drop everything and run in to join me. In the beginning, I used to pick them up and whirl them around, but they're too big for me to do that now.

Some of the dancers, like me, grew up in Mennonite homes. One left her camera off for weeks before she was comfortable letting others see her dance. Another one pulled her retired Mennonite pastor dad into the dance one day, and he said, "This is fun! I should do more of this!" Another one, who wasn't raised Mennonite, was intrigued when she heard about us: "Mennonites... dancing? If the Mennonites can dance, I can dance."

We tried to articulate what the dance meant to us. *It's an active way of being grounded.*

It's a kind of prayer. It's more religious than religion. It gives us permission to be human.

The girls stayed all day, sometimes listening, sometimes reading their books, eating heartily and dancing all the dances. We felt like we were with family, even though we were meeting some of the dancers for the first time.

In the evening, we joined with members of the broader peacebuilding community in the area for a Journey Dance, an hour of guided movement. In the bigger space, with a larger group of people, there was even more energy, but also more exposure. Part of the journey invited us to invent and lead dances. Part of the journey encouraged us to strut our stuff in front of the other dancers. Many of us did not. One of us needed to step outside. I was relieved that the stuff-strutting segment ended before I had to decide to opt out or pretend to enjoy it.

The next day a few of us dancers made it into town for Sunday morning at Shalom Mennonite. We listened to a good, intellectually stimulating sermon. During sharing time, we heard the latest about Gaza, and about opportunities for war tax resisters, and someone's opinion on Warren Buffett's son sending money to Ukraine. For the benedictory song, they pushed back the front row of chairs and Katie and Sue, one of our dancers joining from out of town, invited us up to dance.

There weren't many takers—only the simple people: Irene and I, always emboldened by Sallie's unselfconscious presence. Ella, who checks everyone's name tags at church and will steal your phone if you aren't careful. A few moms and babies eventually came up to sway with us, along with Earl, who is up for anything with his big white beard and booming laugh. But the rest of the kids were away for a storytime, and everyone else at Shalom is too complicated to dance. If Cindy, one of our weekend organizers, had been there, she might have pulled more members of the congregation in—she's a shameless instigator.

There are no points for dancing on the Granola Mennonite scale. There are no negative points for dancing. Dancing is not really part of our equation. It's something we can joke about—an act of rebellion against older Mennonite cultures, maybe—sex might lead to dancing!—but most of our experiences of dancing, if any, come from connections with different cultural contexts, like one of my colleagues, who says he only dances south of the border. Or my mom, who still occasionally dances a few steps of the *cumbia* if the right music comes on, remembering her year abroad in Colombia.

One of the dancers in our group shared that she didn't know how she would have gotten through the pandemic without the dance, waking up to days of "dread and isolation."

Post-pandemic, these are the things I think about when I wake up in the morning: Climate change. Structural racism. Genocide and human rights abuses, and how I'm implicated in them as an American. Protections needed for immigrants and trans kids. Ableism. The books my local school board has banned. All the women and girls in the country who have lost their bodily autonomy. How many guns are in this county. Mass societal delusions perpetuated by algorithms, money, and the worst parts of human nature. That these acres I live on aren't really mine, and that given the privilege of existing here, I should be taking better care of them, making them more productive while at the same time enriching the soil and diversifying the native plants and creatures. That the curriculum I curate at work could make a difference. That it could hurt some people. That I'm not going to get it right all the time, but it would be far worse not to try. That I have more power than I sometimes want to admit, and I shouldn't hide from it. That I need to make a difference, that it's more than my job to make a difference, it's my reason to exist, that the things I do need to count.

It's the orthopraxy, my friend Aili observed. She grew up granola, then came to the Mennonites, so she has some perspective on these things. Mennonites are deeply focused on correct deeds, on what we need to do to be good. Her diagnosis rings true. When it comes to faith, I'm happy to leave the details feathery. Does it even matter if God is a person or an idea, as long as They're part of a good story? Does it matter what faith tradition we come from, as long as we're rooted in it, drawing the good from it, conscious of its shortcomings, having wise conversation with other traditions? But *works*! Friends, this world needs so much work, and we Mennonites are here to do it.

I wake up Mennonite every morning. I need to dance for twenty minutes straight, just so that I can face the day.

Simple as a phone call

A few days after the new *Bluey* episodes, I drop the girls off at the house my parents built for their retirement on a hillside in Hinton, Virginia, when they moved here from Paoli just a few years ago. The front windows face the winter sun, and with the whole house well-insulated (+5) and designed to be centered around the warmth of the woodstove (+5), it is toasty all winter long. Mom gardens flowers, fruit, berries, and vegetables (+3), and Dad builds things, tracking his solar panels (+5) and the level of rainwater in the retention tank he designed (+5). The house is quiet except when a lot of grandchildren chase each other through it, and Dad has time to vacuum as often as he likes, so the floors are spotless. It's a smaller house than it looks from the road, with the walk-in basement adding height, and smaller than it feels inside, with high ceilings and the living and dining spaces flowing together—just two bedrooms, but decks and balconies everywhere (+5).

It is so different from our cluttered, busy, often noisy, complicatedly aging cottage (-5), yet they both feel like home.

Mom greets us at the door, helping to collect snowy boots. Dad is gone today, left early this morning with a busload of Mennonites for a peace action in Washington, D.C. I tried to explain Gaza to Irene in the car this morning. It was complicated. Peace is complicated, too. But some gestures are simple: sharing coffee in a church fellowship hall with hundreds of peace people, sentiments like "Food, not bombs" and "Free the Hostages" painted on signs that look like quilts, choosing a place for nonviolent action based on its good acoustics for singing.

Dad texts me a picture. Eight good Granola Mennonites have come down from Paoli to join the protest, and there's my old church mentor gazing into the camera, and the lyrics to "Simple Song" drift through my mind again.

Jesus and nonviolence, that was what they set out to teach me, I think. But our hidden curriculum exalts simplicity, whether it manifests itself as an aesthetic, as thrift and good stewardship, as having an uncomplicated soul, or as an internalized set of expectations a smart girl carried uncritically for too long.

My parent's house is a haven created on their own terms, a quiet place for any of us to land. It's on one of the first stops of the bus route from the girls' school, and they're almost always available when we need backup. If someone's sick, if I need to schedule a late afternoon meeting, I dial Mom. When it's time to split firewood and Jason needs some extra hands, my dad shows up. When my dad takes a load of trash to the transfer station down in our corner of the county, he calls me—do we have any that needs to go? And when we decided that maybe we're ready to get chickens again this spring (+3), even though we don't have time to build a new coop, Dad said, "Text me the plans."

When I need help, I can call them. I still can hardly believe how simple it is.

Simple like "shputt"

I'm not sure how to spell it, precisely what it means, or even if I found the right word. It's the final vestige of Pennsylvania German used in our household growing up, this fragment of the language of our ancestors. When we were small, Dad would tease us all the time. He would steal our noses, crack imaginary eggs on our heads, mix up his words and pretend to be drunk, and then Mom would laugh and say it was just *shputt*, which to us meant something like nonsense, silliness, joking, play. The only similar word I can find in the Pennsylvania German dictionaries is the verb *shpodda*, to mock. Dad can't clarify either the spelling or meaning of the word, when I text him to ask.

The children embrace shputt intuitively. Sallie gets the slapstick side of shputt; that's why she showed up for breakfast with her panties on her head, why she thinks it's hilarious to transform into Terrible Sallie and try to devour us. Irene is digging into the nuances of humor. When Dad finished building our bespoke chicken house—complete with shingled roof, removable egg boxes, and beautifully stained siding—he hung a sign on it that said "Irene/Sallie's Chicken House." A few days later, he secretly replaced it with a sign that said "Calvin and Hobbes' Chicken House." The twins roared with mingled delight and rage when they discovered it, but after thinking it over a bit, Irene confided to me, "I hope he has some more, different signs, because it wouldn't be very funny to just keep switching between Irene and Sallie and Calvin and Hobbes." Because it's supposed to be a secret, I won't reveal what Dad showed me, hidden in the back of his car. Let's just say there's a trunkload of shputt yet to come.

Shputt helps me think about the kind of simplicity I need for the next half of my life. I do want to keep caring about and helping with all the work of the world. Sometimes that will look like raising chickens and saving money to send for refugees and clearing my schedule so I can get educated and show up for the public comments at the school board or call my senators. And maybe sometimes that will look like dancing and eating frozen Dino Nuggets and making bad jokes about Mennonite cookbooks so that we can get through this day, and the next one, and the next one, with joy.

I'm pretty sure that this kind of writing, like dancing, doesn't even show up on the Granola Mennonite Scorecard, or won't until I learn to rewrite my internal scorecard. Maybe someday I will write a book that penetrates the marrow of a social problem in a transformative way (+5). And maybe this is the only one I'll ever write, relevant to a rather limited audience of Granola Mennonites (plus the folks who picked up this book hoping to find recipes and had the patience to read to the end). Dear reader, I hope it made you laugh at yourself, or at us, and maybe it helped you see yourself better or with more compassion, a time or two. I think that might be enough.

Gratitudes

First, thank you, dear reader, for your precious time, from your own wild life. If you're a Granola Mennonite, thank you for understanding. If you stumbled upon this book seeking recipes, here at last is your reward: one real recipe, the granola we eat at our house. It's adapted from Jennifer Murch, whose Granola Mennonite bona fides include cheesemaker, cow owner, and unschooler. We use only honey for sweetener in our version since we still have plenty left from the bees, and this is already doubled so there's enough to give away. At Christmas, we use craisins instead of raisins. For nuts, we prefer to use pecans. (The land where Jason's grandfather and my great-grandfather were long-ago neighbors in Denbigh, Virginia, had towering pecan trees on it, so we're partial to them.)

Peanut Butter and Honey Granola
- Preheat oven to 250 degrees.
- Toss together in a large roaster:
    - 10 cups rolled oats
    - 2-4 cups chopped nuts—almonds or pecans
    - 2 cups coconut
    - 1/2 teaspoon salt
- Combine and warm in a saucepan or microwave-safe bowl, stirring until smooth:
    - 1 cup honey
    - 1 cup peanut butter
- Pour the wet ingredients over the dry ones, and stir to com-

bine. You may need to squish a bit with your fingers to get the lumps out. Or leave them in. The lumps are the best part.
- Bake for 90 minutes, stirring every 20-30 minutes. You have to use a wooden spoon to do this. Don't ask me why. It doesn't feel right if you use a metal spoon.
- Allow to cool. Add:
  ◦ 2 cup raisins
- Store in glass jars.

Thanks to Michael A. King, publisher of this book and some of my earliest pieces. I still remember the thrill of that first acceptance in *Dreamseeker Magazine*. To DreamSeeker Memoir Series editor Jeff Gundy, for encouraging me to submit to this series years ago, for your reassuring wisdom, and for turning around my manuscripts with such speed it sometimes gave me whiplash. Thanks also to Gwen Stamm, designer, and Tiffany Showalter, photographer, for helping me realize my dream of a chicken-centric cover. Thank you, Kate Baer, for permission to use lines from "Moon Song" from your marvelous collection *What Kind of Woman* as the epigraph.

Thanks to my family and Jason's family featured in this book. In honor of my Grandmother Janet Elizabeth Weaver Yoder, I include full names because, as she often told me, the people of my generation need to understand how satisfying it is to people of her generation to be able to figure out how we connect to the people they know: Grammy Janet and Grandpa Morris Harvey Yoder, Grandpa Claude Raymond Beachy and Edna Yoder Beachy; my dad James Conrad Beachy (not to be mistaken for either of the other two Jim Beachys living in the Valley) and mom Bonnie Jo Yoder Beachy; Jason's father Harold Lowell Alderfer and mother Elaine Marie Erb.

Thanks to the Mennonite church communities on the Warwick River, in Paoli, in Philippi, and and to dear Shalom who nurtured a love of singing, poetry, mountain hikes, service, and potlucks. Thanks to all of you brilliant Granola Mennonites, church and college friends, who overwhelm me with your devotion to good works and local produce.

To professors and committee members in the West Virginia University MFA program: Gail and Tim Adams, Mark Brazaitis, Sara Pritchard, and Ethel Morgan Smith. Kevin Oderman, who got me writing about martyrs in his creative nonfiction class. To classmates, who continue to inspire me as I read your books and your social media posts.

Thanks to the smart girls of Paoli, Indiana, who stayed connected and shared stories, good memes, and twin hacks over the years: Espri and Jaime—and Jordana, still present in so many ways. To our English teacher Ruth Uyesugi.

To the Mennonite/s Writing community—especially Jeff and Julia Spicher Kasdorf for pulling me into the earlier martyr book project, *Tongue Screws and Testimonies*—and Jean Janzen, for that early undergrad poetry class at EMU, and Ann Hostetler for running the most recent conference at Goshen that inspired a 2 a.m. proposal for this book, and Cheryl Denise Miller for hospitality, road trip companionship, seeing me in a poem when I was barely old enough to see myself, and telling me enough about your publishing experience with Cascadia to generate a productive envy within me.

To the folks from the valley who helped with my writing, the Shenandoah Valley Inkslingers in various iterations, particularly Aili Huber, Anna Maria Johnson, Andrew Jenner, Chad Gusler, Jennifer Murch, and Jessica Penner.

To Jeremy Nafziger who reviewed a book manuscript a decade ago made up of the first half of all this, and Michael Ann Courtney who helped me with long-ago MFA applications and let me audit her epic poetry course.

To my own Mennonite institution, Eastern Mennonite University, for release time for writing and funding for some weekend retreats. To former professors Carroll Yoder and Jay B. Landis in Language and Literature at EMU and to my directors in the same program, Vi Dutcher and Kevin Seidel, who helped me carve out precious writing time.

To the people who kept me sane on Zoom through the season of this book's creation, Katie and all the resilient dancers, and to cousins Katrina and Holly for the evening hangouts.

To Mom, who gave us the precious gift of Story, who is without question the reason I'm a reader and a writer. To Dad, who encouraged me to use my voice, and to big sister Elizabeth, for all the first stories we invented together, and for showing me the way.

To Irene and Sallie, for being your wonderful selves and generating such good material and creative energy all day long.

And thank you to Jason, my Farmboy Mennonite, for cheering on the work, holding down the fort during my writing retreats, and most importantly, living this life with me. The word cloud I generated from this book manuscript says, in the largest words, "One time, Jason." I love you.

Credits

"Me and the Martyrs" originally published in *The Tusculum Review* (2007); reprinted in *Center for Mennonite Writing Journal* (2009) and *Tongue Screws and Testimonies: Poems, Stories, and Essays Inspired by the Martyrs Mirror* (Herald Press, 2010).

"Amish Country" and "Notes to Myself" published in *Dreamseeker Magazine* (2005).

"Selling the Farm" published in *Shenandoah* (2009).

"A Butcher of Conscience" (2008) and "Walking" (2011) originally published in *The Tusculum Review;* "The Last Worker" published in *The Tusculum Review* online (2009).

"Field Notes Towards a Doctrine of Chickens" published in *The Cresset* (2011).

"Notes from the Night Owl Feed" published as a book chapter in *On Mothering Multiples: Complexities and Possibilities.* Ed. Kathy Mantas. Demeter Press. 2016.

"Eggs: A Short History of Infertility and Ducks" published in *The Cresset* (Lent 2014).

"Lavish Banquets" (2012) and "Woman Built of Stones: A Mother Tries to Write" (2023) published in *The Journal of Mennonite Writing.*

"Milk" published as a book chapter in *Mennonite Mothering.* Co-editors, Rachel Epp Buller and Kerry Fast. Demeter Press. 2013.

"Mennonite Girls Can Read (With Recipes!)" published as short fiction in *Mennonite Life* (Summer 2012).

Notes

1. For those Mennonite readers seeking to contextualize this chapter using the time-honored practice of hymnal dating (like tree-rings, but more musical), please note that at the time of writing in the early 2000s we still considered the blue *Hymnal: A Worship Book* (1992, published jointly by Brethren and Mennonite Presses) to be new. And, yes, if you're doing the math, that places me among the last Gen Xers, a year older and centuries wiser than the Geriatric Millennials. And yes, now we have the new new hymnal, the purple book, still so fresh off the press as I edit this work in 2023 that I haven't learned the new number for 606.
2. From "Why I Do Not Cease Teaching and Writing," 1539. Trans. 1871 John F. Funk.
3. Introduction to Harvey Hostetler, *Descendants of Barbara Hochstedler and Christian Stutzman* (Berlin, Ohio: Gospel Book Store, 1998), first printed in 1938.
4. Virgil Miller, *Both Sides of the Ocean: Amish Mennonites from Switzerland to America* (Morgantown, Pa.: Masthof Press, 2002).
5. A friend insists that I explain scrapple. Where to begin? It's the stuff of nightmares or the food of the gods, depending on your tastes. Scraps of pig, cornmeal, sage, fried in a crispy slab and served, according to taste, with ketchup, apple butter, maple syrup, or nothing. For the many Swiss-German Mennonites who didn't take a century-long detour through Russia before migrating to America, it's an answer to borscht, vareniki, and other dishes that remain mysterious to us.
6. Emmert F. Bittinger, ed. and David Rodes and Norman Wenger, compilers, *Unionists and the Civil War Experience in the Shenandoah Valley*, vol. 3. (Dayton, Va.: Valley Research Associates, 2003), 222.
7. The new, now old, blue one, of course.
8. Do I need to make it clear, dear readers, that this correspondence and the entire collection of recipes is entirely apocryphal? I've had

only good experiences with Mennonite publishers. I suppose I was responding to the market sensation and squicky title of *Mennonite Girls Can Cook* when I wrote this. The most far-fetched idea in the whole thing is that I'd write a book of essays on theopoetics and Mennonite literary history. I did not tell the truth in this essay, but I hope I made it interesting. If you attempt to make any of these recipes, please do not invite me for dinner.

9. In tribute to Maggie Smith's poem, "Small Shoes."

10. Credit to the late disability rights advocate Stella Young for the term "inspiration porn."

The Author

Kirsten Eve Beachy lives with her husband Jason Alderfer, twin daughters Irene and Sallie, Sophie the cat, and a half-dozen unruly hens in Briery Branch, Virginia, where she writes about motherhood, disability, and changelings. Kirsten was born in Goshen, Indiana, and attends Shalom Mennonite Congregation in Harrisonburg, Virginia. She received degrees in Philosophy and Theology and Theater from Eastern Mennonite University and an MFA in creative writing from West Virginia University. Kirsten now serves as director of the Core Curriculum and teaches creative writing and journalism at Eastern Mennonite University.

Kirsten edited the anthology *Tongue Screws and Testimonies: Poems, Stories, and Essays Inspired by the Martyrs Mirror* (Herald Press, 2010) and co-chaired Mennonites Writing VI: Solos and Harmonies, a binational writing conference at EMU (2012). Her stories, poems, and essays appear in *Shenandoah, Wrath-Bearing Tree, The Cresset, Center for Mennonite Writing Journal, The Tusculum Review, Relief: a Quarterly Christian Expression, Rhubarb, Dreamseeker*, and three anthologies: *Hint Fiction* (Norton, 2010), *Mennonite Mothering* (Demeter, 2013), and *On Mothering Multiples: Complexities and Possibilities* (Demeter, 2016). For more information on her current projects or to connect on social media, visit her author blog at kirstenevebeachy.wordpress.com.